Make Money at Home

The Mini-business Handbook

Also by Gordon Wells:

How to Communicate

The Successful Author's Handbook

The Magazine Writer's Handbook
The Book Writer's Handbook
The Craft of Writing Articles
The Craft of Effective Letter Writing
Writer's Questions Answered

Traffic Engineering
Comprehensive Transport Planning

Make Money at Home

The Mini-business Handbook

Gordon Wells

foulsham
LONDON • NEW YORK • TORONTO • SYDNEY

foulsham
Yeovil Road, Slough, Berkshire SL1 4JH.

ISBN 0-572-01667-0

Copyright © Gordon Wells 1991

All rights reserved.

The Copyright Act (1956) prohibits (subject to certain very limited exceptions) the making of copies of any copyright work or of a substantial part of such a work, including the making of copies by photocopying or similar process. Written permission to make a copy or copies must therefore normally be obtained from the publisher in advance. It is advisable to consult the publisher if in any doubt as to the legality of any copying which is to be undertaken.

Photoset by Typesetting Solutions, Slough, Berks.
Printed in Great Britain by St. Edmundsbury Press,
Bury St. Edmunds, Suffolk.

CONTENTS

1 Introduction   9

What mini-business? Motivation. Mini-business qualities. Your commitment. Money. The alternative.

2 A business plan   25

Types of business. The plan itself. Business objectives. Market assessment. Capital resources and requirements. The profit plan. The cash-flow forecast. Monitoring.

3 You — the prime mover   49

Family relationships. Planning your time. Priorities and targets. Being your own boss.

4 Premises and equipment   63

Planning considerations. Accommodation options. Specific equipment. Office equipment. The office computer. Word processing. Choosing a computer. Programs. Other office equipment. An office system.

5 *The end product or service*   93
Selling. Marketing policy. Packaging the product. Your business image. Your personal image.

6 *Marketing the product — advertising*   111
Contacts. Sales letters. Follow-up by phone. Brochures. Mechanics of mailing. Advertising. Using the press.

7 *Effective letter writing*   135
Planning your letters. A letter structure. Clear simple writing. Writing that sounds right. Polishing. Be unimpressive.

8 *Selling face to face*   153
Good presence. Good product. Good presentation.

9 *Making a presentation*   167
Thinking about talking. Preparing a talk. Practicing your talk. Delivering a talk. Visual aids.

10 *Money — and related matters*   181
Grants. Accounts. Insurance. Income Tax. National Insurance contributions. Value Added Tax (VAT). Pensions.

Case Studies
23, 46, 90, 109, 132, 150, 164

Index   *203*

ACKNOWLEDGEMENTS

I would like to record my grateful thanks to Jerry Marchant for vetting Chapter 10 for me, and for making so many helpful comments thereon. The correctness of that chapter owes much to him; any remaining faults are my own responsibility.

I am also most grateful to the mini-business people who so kindly bared their innermost secrets and responded so helpfully to the questionnaire from which I developed the Case Studies. They remain anonymous — but they know who they are.

Gordon Wells

1
INTRODUCTION

If you want to work as a freelance — a freelance *anything* — this book is for you. If you have recently retired, or have just been offered early retirement, this book is for you.

If you have a creative hobby or spare-time activity and would like to work at it full-time, this book is definitely for you. If you long to work for yourself —and not to have a boss breathing down your neck all the time — again, this book is for you.

You're going to start a one-person mini-business. That is, you're going to set up, in a small way, a business for yourself. Just you. You're going to be your own boss — and your own paymaster.

You must be prepared to work hard. You've got to be just as tough a boss — on yourself — as your old boss ever was. (But at least it'll be you being tough on you.) This one-person mini-business of yours is going to be no rest-cure. But it's a great life!

Let's start by defining the ground rules. This book is about how to make money, working from home. It is not about how to make a fortune. You probably won't. Few of us do. But you could make a good living.

It's about how to work for yourself; how to set up your own one-person mini business. And that "one-person" is an important qualification. The book is *not* about partnerships, or setting up a small business and employing staff. It's about a MINI-BUSINESS.

These comments about staff however, are not meant to preclude casual helpers or the part-time assistance of a spouse (in this instance, usually a wife — and this is my only chauvinistic comment in this book). If your spouse works part-time for you, but is paid less than the personal tax allowance and less than the lower limit for National Insurance contributions, this can be highly efficient. But don't try to "fiddle" this, it must be a real employment.

(Your mini-business of course, may grow to such an extent that, in time, you will need to employ staff. And good luck to you. This book does not deal with "being a boss", nor with the extra work (PAYE, National Insurance contributions, etc.) or the problems that this can lead to. Nothing suggested in this book though will hinder such growth — nor worsen the problems that come with a work-force.)

Before we go any further though, let us contemplate our navels. We'll only do this once; after this chapter it'll all be "hard" advice. To make a success of a mini-business though, you need to start by thinking — carefully — about:

- what you are going to do; (What *can* you do, and is there a market, a demand, for this?)
- what you are getting into; (Do you have any idea what the life of a self-employed person is like? Have you the right motivation? Can you stand the strain?)
- whether you have the makings of a "mini-business-person";
- how to cope with the financial side; (You may need capital; you will certainly need enough "day-to-day money" to keep you going while you are starting up.)

and:

- the alternative. (What if you *don't* start your own mini-business?)

What mini-business?

The first thing you have to establish is just what sort of a mini-business you are going to get into. For many people this will be easy. If you are a skilled computer programmer, an experienced consultant in any profession, a potter, or even a writer, you already know what you want to do. But if you don't already have an existing commitment, hobby or skill you need to give this matter careful thought.

After all, you can't just open up a shop; you need something to sell, something to put in the window.

So, a little more soul-searching is called for. Sit down and think about what sort of mini-business you are going to get into. To start you thinking — and inevitably, the omissions from this list far outweigh those included, which are offered merely as examples — some possibilities are:

Professional: management consultant, accountant, computer programmer, PR services, office services, engineer, architect, teacher, solicitor, journalist, etc..

Creative: Artist, photographer, sculptor, writer, musician, and a variety of general crafts-persons.

Entrepreneur: Import/Export agent, insurance broker, caterer, restaurateur, and any general sales activity (even car boot sales operations)

Skilled workers: Gardener, window cleaner, cook, nanny, butler, vehicle mechanic, "Mr Fixit", etc. (Many workers in eg the building and construction industry choose to be self-employed.)

(And yes, of course those classifications are quite ridiculous: some journalists are very creative, a good photographer is surely professional, a nanny is clearly more than just a skilled worker, a . . . But however I classified them would be wrong, so let me just apologise to everyone, in advance.)

The choice of mini-business occupation is yours. I know of one man who took up carpentry as a middle-age hobby and developed it into a retirement mini-business; another colleague retired after a lifetime of cerebral (management) work, and happily became a self-employed gardener; a lot of my friends (I too, since retiring) work happily and with varying success as full-time writers; many computer programmers work as well-paid self-employed contractors; one-person solicitors' or accountants' mini-businesses abound. And many people run small "shops" on their own — often from home, using their car boots.

Having chosen an activity for your mini-business, you next need to consider whether there is any *scope* there — ie, in that activity, with your ability, *and* in your geographical location — for you to run a profitable business. A writer who never gets anything other than rejections, is not going to make a success of a writing mini-business — anywhere. A mini-business set up to supply lunchtime sandwiches to workers is unlikely to make a profit, if it is located in a remote rural area.

You may propose to make the most attractively carved ivory bed-post knobs imaginable — but how many people will want to buy them? Will they beat a path to your Central London, (or Lake District) door? And even if they do, what price will they pay? Is it worth your while producing them if that is all the return you get?

Think hard — and realistically — about your chances. We will look in more detail at market study in a later chapter.

Motivation

You have thought about what to do, and whether or not it could be a viable proposition; now what about you and your family. Do you realise what you might be letting yourself in for?

Life in a mini-business is not like the life of the average wage-slave. It differs in several important ways; in a mini-business you need:

- to produce saleable work — again and again;
- a financial buffer;
- to be economical;
- to come up with *ideas*;
- to get on with people.

As a wage-slave, you can stop for a while and chat to a colleague — about last night's TV or the latest political scandal — you'll still get paid. You can spend all day in an unproductive meeting — and even then you'll still get paid. In a mini-business you get paid only for what you produce. No product, no pay.

As a wage-slave, you know — more-or-less for certain — that a pay cheque will arrive at the end of each month; it won't come late. In a mini-business, even if you've earnt the money, you never really know when you'll get paid. You need a financial buffer — money in the bank — to safeguard you against late payment.

As a wage-slave you can be extravagant with stationery, etc. — "there's plenty more where that came from." You don't need to worry — apart from cursing the inconvenience — if your computer goes down; the service engineer will soon be there to sort it out. In a mini-business you watch the pennies — because they're your own. You will learn to be economical with stationery. You will insure your own equipment against breakdown. And when it's out of action, and you have to sit and wait for the repairman, you will soon realise that it's you who is losing money — not "the firm".

As a wage-slave, if you can't think what to do next, your boss will soon tell you. Ideas are a bonus. In a mini-business you must always have something new up your sleeve. You can't stand still.

As a wage-slave, if you have a row with the person in charge of the drawing office, or wherever, you avoid them. If you can't stand one of the clients, there's a fair chance that someone else can take that one on for you. In a one-person mini-business, if you fall out with one of your contacts, it could well mean that the market is closed to you. You need to be your own PR person — and on duty all the time.

Life in your own mini-business is no bed of roses. It's hard work. Before you jump into it, search your soul for your true reasons for making the choice.

Let's be a little bit pessimistic, and explore them. What do you want out of life — life in a mini-business?

Security? A mini-business is seldom secure in its early years. Quite a few mini-businesses fail — through lack of preparation, lack of capital, lack of drive, lack of business acumen, etc. A mini-business is a gamble — how big a gamble depends on your personal circumstances. (In my case, as a writer, my financial investment is no more than the cost of my computer — for word processing — and a camera; and I *could* live without my writing income. So, a very small gamble. Some mini-business gambles are much bigger.)

Status? People will "think far more of you" if you have a big company car than if you have a "self-paid-for" mini-car. There is seldom any status in running a mini-business. (Unless you are Catherine Cookson or David Bailey.)

Money? Yes, maybe. Many people with succesful mini-businesses make a lot of money — but there are also those who make very little. (I have twenty published non-fiction books; I would hate to have to live on the royalties alone. I have to keep writing — to pay for the daily caviar.)

Home life? If you are working from home, clearly you will be closer to your family than if you are commuting to London every day. But you may not actually be able to spend more free time with the family — you could well be working longer hours than the average wage-slave. Without doubt, when you first set up your mini-business you will *want* to work 25 hours in every 24.

You may also need — or wish — to involve the family in the business. Many a wife does duty as unpaid secretary, book-keeper, or telephonist. And teenagers *can* be trained to answer the phone properly — particularly if their next holiday depends on it. (You may be better off paying your wife though — *see* later.) but at least you'll have all that *togetherness*.

Time off? Yes, of course. But every moment you take off is lost income. When you were a wage-slave you got paid holidays; in a mini-business you don't. Initially though, if you're keen — and you must be — you will find yourself unwilling to take time off.

But enough of that. The biggest plus about a mini-business is that you are working for yourself. If you make a success of it, you — and only you (and yours) — get the advantage. And with luck, all your hard work will pay off. Just don't think of it as a sinecure.

Mini-business qualities

We have looked at the "down" side, the "black" side of operating a mini-business. And we have recognised that it is not for everyone. But you think it is right for you.

To be a successful mini-business-person you need to possess — or develop — certain personal qualities. The most important of these are:

- drive and determination — a will to succeed
- tenacity — an unwillingness to give up
- resilience — a refusal to be beaten
- competitiveness — a wish to do better than others.

All these qualities are much related. If you have one, you probably have the rest too. It is also essential, but this book will help you to develop this, to have:

- "pushiness" — a willingness to get out and *sell*.

And, last but most certainly not least, you need to shed any ideas you may have about what jobs you will do, and what jobs are for minions, the more junior staff. You will no longer have any "more junior staff". You're on your own. YOU alone are the post-boy, the typist, the messenger, the salesman, the receptionist, the telephone operator, even the "sweeper-up". If you need it, you're it. So, the last of the qualities that you need is:

- versatility — the willingness and ability to turn your hand to any and every job in the mini-business book.

Figure 1.1 The pros and cons of starting a mini-business

CHECKLIST

Con   **Pro**

No   *Yes*

Con		Pro
☐	Do you have a creative hobby or craft? (Anything from carpentry, through lacemaking to writing)	✓
☐	Do you work in a potentially one-person profession? (Accountancy, graphic design, PR, etc.)	✓
☐	Have you already set yourself up with all the necessary equipment? (Potter's wheel, writer's word-processor, photographer's dark-room, etc.)	✓

☐	Do you know what you want to do?	☐
☐	Do you have something to sell?	✓
☐	Do you enjoy selling things? (Either as your job, or when disposing of no-longer-wanted items.)	✓
☐	Do you *really* want to work for yourself?	✓
☐	Do you long to escape from the constraints of working for a boss?	✓
☐	Are you a "self-starter" — someone who doesn't have to be told what to do?	✓
☐	Do you have lots of good ideas for making money?	✓
☐	Are you prepared to work "all hours" at your mini-business?	✓
☐	Do you get on well with people? (It is no good starting up a mini-business just to be alone.)	✓
☐	Do you have a spare room, or corner of a room, at home, with a telephone?	✓

Do you have a pension?

✓   OR   ☐

Do you have a working spouse/partner? (Just as good.)

Have you enough capital to cover the start-up expenses of your mini-business?

☐   OR   ✓

Can you make a good case, to your bank manager, for a start-up loan (and "eating money" too)?

Figure 1.1 is a checklist from which you can assess the pros and cons of starting a mini-business — relating them specifically to yourself.

Your commitment

One of the first ways to develop, and to demonstrate, your fitness for running your mini-business is to convince yourself that you are going to succeed.

You need to *make a commitment*. All those — usually American — self-development or management *gurus* and Bible-thumping evangelists have, in this sense, the right idea. They get you to make a public commitment to your objective, or to your belief. Once you've made that commitment, you will try harder to stick to it.

Well-known romantic novelist, Mary Wibberley, tells us in her book, *To Writers With Love* (Buchan & Enright, 1985) how she made a successful commitment. "I found a notebook, and wrote in it in bold black capitals: 'I AM GOING TO WRITE A BOOK AND GET IT PUBLISHED.' Somehow, that set the seal on it. It became a challenge, a fact waiting to be accomplished." It took Mary seven years and the addition of the words "BY MILLS AND BOON" to succceed, but succeed she did. Now she has forty-odd Mills & Boon books to her credit — and has probably made a great deal of money.

You should decide on your own mini-business ambition and set it down on paper. I believe it is a good idea to pin this statement of your target to a wall somewhere where you will see it regularly. (In the toilet perhaps?)

One thing you must learn if you are to establish your successful mini-business though is not to give up at the first — or second or 25th — obstacle.

You will soon find out that by no means all of your marvellous ideas actually come off. You will write letters to contacts, seeking work: few will bother to reply. You will get past that stage and believe you have sold a project or idea — then suddenly it all goes quiet. You hear no more. but you must still keep at it. Some of your efforts will pay off. One day, one will pay off big — and your mini-business will really take off. Then you'll have too much work.

When I write my non-fiction books, I sell the idea of the book before I write it. I offer a synopsis and a sample chapter to a carefully selected publisher and ask for a contract.

Some years ago, one after the other, nine supposedly "carefully selected" publishers turned down one of my book ideas. The tenth persuaded me to change the *slant* of the synopsis a little — and then commissioned the book. It went, successfully, into two editions. That was *How to Communicate* (McGraw-Hill, 2nd edition, 1986).

If I had given up at the first, second or even the ninth rejection, that book would never have been published. I *knew* there was a market for it (I'd just got the market a bit wrong); and I worked hard at selling it.

You have got to have faith — self-confidence — tenacity, and "pushiness" to make a success of any mini-business.

Over the years, I have offered one other book idea to over forty publishers. On that one, I really have just about given up. It's still a good idea. But it seems there is no market for it. Market study is looked at in more detail later in this book. It is a vitally important part of every mini-business.

Money

The ideal time to set up a mini-business — well, one of the ideal times anyway — is on retirement. Early or full-term, retirement nearly always means a pension: something to live on. And with the comfort of knowing where your — and your partner's — next meal is coming from, you can work at your mini-business with a clear conscience. All you need do is ensure that you are not putting your pension in jeopardy.

For some mini-businesses you will also need capital. Capital to purchase expensive equipment perhaps, to publicise the services you have to offer, or to build up a basic stock of goods to sell. At the outset, you must stop and think about this need for capital.

On retirement, you may well have a lump sum — a long-service gratuity — that you can use. Is your mini-business the *right* use of that money? Otherwise, you may need to borrow money from the bank. Not only will you have to pay for that privilege, but you will also have to satisfy the bank manager that it is a sensible investment. Satisfy yourself first.

If you are setting up a mini-business other than on retirement, you must also make provision for "eating money" until the business is established. You need to think about your *cash flow*. (You may get plenty of work and send out lots of invoices — bills — but payment is often very slow. You might expect payment at the end of the month — but, as often as not, it will be a month later still.) You still have the mortgage payments to keep up and the food bills to meet.

We look more closely into the financial aspects of starting a mini-business in the next chapter. And, of course, not all mini-businesses need capital; for many self-employed occupations there is no need for start-up finance.

The alternative

Once you have sat down and had a really good think about your mini-business you may have lost some of your commitment. That is part of the reason for sitting down and thinking. It is far better to get cold feet now, before you take the plunge, than when it's too late. Of course, I hope you are even more firmly determined to go ahead. But if you really have got cold feet, is there perhaps an alternative to just giving up the whole idea?

Yes, there is. And it's a good one. It's how I started.

You can keep on working as a nine-to-five wage-slave and start your mini-business in your "spare" time. Build it up into a viable, but perhaps still small, concern while you have the financial security of a full-time job. Then, with the confidence of having run the mini-business successfully in your spare time, you can take the plunge and go full-time.

As a writer for instance, it is likely that you will attract a lot of rejections while learning the trade. I started writing — for money — about forty years ago. Over the years, I collected scores of rejection slips — but I gradually built up my expertise and my writing earnings.

About twenty years ago I had a major career change; I was retired — with a small but immediate pension. I toyed with the idea then of writing full time. But my liking for comfort, good food and drink, and relative security led to my seeing sense — and continuing to write in my spare time only. Today, I have the added financial security of a second, larger, pension — and I am still young enough to run my now-thriving mini-business. I have the best of all worlds. And I believe that my mini-business does much to keep me feeling young.

There is a great deal to be said for a part-time mini-business. It's even harder work than a full-time one; but it is *SAFE*; and you can build it up slowly and steadily — you are not desperate for the money.

Specific advantages of establishing a mini-business in your "spare time", whilst remaining in full-time employment, include:
- You will have a more comfortable financial "buffer" than a pension: you can live on your income as a wage-slave while building up the profit-making poten-

tial of the mini-business. You will be able to "learn the trade" in greater financial comfort too.
- Depending on your salary level, you may not be required to pay further National Insurance contributions on your *part-time* mini-business activities. (*See* Chapter 10 for more details about National Insurance.)
- You can determine — with relative accuracy — the likely viability of your proposed mini-business. You *may* be kidding yourself — the world may not be just waiting to beat a path to your door. A writer, for instance, who collects nothing but rejection slips, would be wise to continue writing in his or her spare time, until successful. Wishing won't make it so.
- You can equip yourself with all the necessary capital equipment before you go into business "for real". (But financial principles outlined in the next chapter — about ensuring a realistic financial return on your capital investment — will still apply.)
- You can get used to working alone.

If for some reason you are not able to stay on at work and run your mini-business in your spare time, there is another practical alternative. You can find a job working for a small firm in the same line of business as you plan.

That way, you can gain invaluable experience of working practices. And if you show a real interest, the boss may show you some of the secrets of how the business actually works. A possible spin-off benefit too could be the offer of a partnership in the firm. This would no longer be, by our definition, a mini-business, but it would offer many of the same advantages.

Whatever you do though — whether working the business up on a part-time basis, or gaining relevant experience while still working for someone else — don't give up on your commitment. Your mini-business WILL work.

CASE STUDY – *Roy*

Roy started his writing and publishing bureau jsut a year ago, in his fifties. He works full-time, and operates as a "sole trader". Subject to ethical considerations, he is prepared to write anything — advertising copy, magazine articles (but with no firm guarantee of publication), sales letters, speeches or CVs, even the minutes of meetings.

He had made no advance preparation for setting up his mini-business: he lost a senior job in the publishing/advertising world and, doubting that he could get anything similar at his age, opted for self-employment.

Operating from a couple of rooms at home, Roy has equipped himself well, but frugally, for his mini-business. He has a telephone with answering machine, a typewriter — recently, a word-processor too (an Amstrad PCW 9512) — and a fax machine. That's all he needs. Total start-up cost, under £1000 — which meant he needed no bank loan. He had a small amount of "separation money" from his previous employment — but no pension. (He is now buying a self-employed pension.)

Wisely, before he started up, Roy discussed his business proposals with his bank, who gave him much helpful advice. He also took advice from a good accountant. He prepared an initial 6-month cash-flow forecast, but not a formal business plan.

The first year of his mini-business was a success. His income, after all expenses, was around £15,000. (Expenses are by no means minimal, even in a word-based mini-business; first-year receipts were more than twice the final income.) In that first year though, Roy depended for much of his work on two or three large clients. But one of these has just pulled out —through no fault of Roy's — and he is now struggling again; he had not succeeded in broadening his base sufficiently, nor quickly enough.

He now realises that he needs a solid base of a larger number of clients with a steady flow of repeat requirements. And clients like that are hard to find in the "made to measure" words business.

Roy is once again — indeed, it's an ongoing exercise — busily seeking clients. He gets work by personal recommendations, by approaching contacts from his past, and by a small, ongoing, display advertisement in a few carefully targeted business magazines and papers. He follows up responses to the advertisement with a really good, hard-selling letter. He will surely overcome the loss of that major client. But it takes time. He has also had some unexpected luck. A leading magazine recently published a quite unsolicited news item about his business.

He is optimistic and, for those in similar circumstances, would recommend a mini-business such as his. Roy's advice, to those about to start their own mini-business, is:
- keep costs to a minimum;
- accept that time spent on filing, systems, accounts, etc., is seldom wasted;
- avoid wasting your own (valuable, skilled) time doing things that others can do for you —better and cheaper;
- get a good, qualified, strait-laced, accountant.

2
A BUSINESS PLAN

We have already established, in the previous chapter, that you are determined to start up a mini-business. And you have assured yourself that you have the right attitude, the right qualities — and the *commitment* — to be a successful mini-business-person. Now let's think about the money side.

The purpose of any business is . . . to make money. There is no point in your investing all that effort, and money, in a mini-business, only to get nothing back. As Robert Townsend, one-time Chairman of Avis Rent-a-Car, wrote in his famous management book, *Up the Organisation*, "If you're not in business for fun or profit, what the hell are you doing here?" My only criticism of that comment is that I think it should have been "fun *and* profit".

Accepting then that you are in business to make at least a small profit, you need a Business Plan. You can't just leave things to chance. Merely hoping for the best won't make it so.

Before we look at what a business plan is though, let us clarify the sort of mini-business you will be in.

Types of business

Setting up your own mini-business, there are only three ways of operating, three possibilities:

- as a sole trader
- within a partnership
- as a limited liability company.

The sole trader: Alone, you can start up in business immediately, without legal formalities or start-up costs. The sole trader can even employ other people. (But then it might not fall within our preferred description — *see* page 9 — of what we mean in this book by a mini-business.) The only legal requirements of a sole trader are that he/she keep proper accounts for tax purposes and, if the business is big enough, register for VAT. (*See* Chapter 10.) A sole trader is not obliged to register a trading name — which need not be his/her own.

The only real (and in some instances, by no means insignificant) disadvantage is that the sole trader's liability is unlimited: this means that if you get into debt, all of your personal assets can be called upon to meet the debt. (So, play it safe and consider transferring your house etc into your wife's name.)

The partnership: It would not be wise to enter into a partnership — even with a spouse — without a formal legal agreement setting out the personal responsibilities and liabilities of each partner. That apart, a partnership is a particularly viable arrangement for establishing a business. As with a sole trader, a partnership is not obliged to register its trading name. The disadvantages are that all the partners (and a partnership is not restricted to only two partners) are responsible for all debts incurred by the partnership — unless otherwise specified.

It is possible to set up a *limited partnership* in which one or more partners is committed to only a limited liability. If, in a legal agreement, a partner specifies a limited financial liability of a particular sum, then that partner is not liable for debts exceeding that amount. (Any partnership agreement should also specify the arrangements for sharing of profits and the arrangements for winding up the partnership — yes, even of husband and wife. It can happen.)

The limited company: The company becomes the trading entity. Don't try to establish a limited company yourself; it can be done, but it is more sensible to approach a solicitor and, with his/her assistance, buy a ready-made company "off the shelf". A limited company has to have two named Directors; there is much to be said for employing your solicitor as the Company Secretary.

If you don't like the name of the off-the-shelf company, you can easily apply — to the Registrar of Companies — to change it, or you can simply trade under a different name — "XYZ Toilets Ltd, trading as Graphic Antiques". And there are two important "plus points": it is usually easier for a limited company to borrow money; and, should the company go into debt, your financial liabilities are limited to the extent of your share holding.

Accounting requirements for a limited company are more onerous than for a sole trader or partnership; the accounts have to be audited; the annual reports must be publicly disclosed (by depositing with the Registrar of Companies).

Against that, as a limited company you can employ yourself, and give yourself such tax *perks* as a company car — which you cannot indulge in as a sole trader. But if you do employ yourself, you also get into all the hassle of employing staff, which, we decided in Chapter 1, is best avoided.

There is no doubt that sole trader operation is far and away the simplest, most convenient way of establishing what we have defined as a mini-business. Throughout this book we shall assume sole trader operation. In that context — the business plan.

The plan itself

First, let us specify what we mean by a business plan. A business plan is a written statement of what your mini-business is going to do, how it is going to do it, and the financial effects of so doing. Because you need to prepare this business plan before you start, it is all a question of forward planning — of looking ahead. And everyone knows the problems of looking into a crystal ball. (Two deep breaths and everything clouds over.)

More specifically, a business plan consists of:

- a clear definition of the objectives of the mini-business and the capabilities of the boss-person — you.
- an assessment of the market for your product or service — and how you propose to reach that market.
- a statement of the capital sums needed for or involved in the mini-business — and their sources.
- a profit plan — a comparison of your sales receipts and your expenses.
- a cash flow forecast — it is not enough to know that receipts exceed expenses if the income is so delayed as to entail your having to borrow "eating money". The cost of borrowing will affect your profit plan.

And before I go into further detail about the content of the business plan I can already hear you "switching off". "I'm only going to be working for myself, doing a bit of lecturing (or whatever) in my spare time. I don't need all that fuss." But you're wrong. As we said at the start of this chapter, you're in business — even your little mini-business — to make a profit. (If not, as above, "What the hell are you here for?")

A business plan will also help you identify those parts of your proposed mini-business that are likely to be the most profitable. To illustrate: I write books and I lecture.

For a book, I sign a contract before I start writing and get a few hundred pounds "up front". (An advance of royalties "on signature".) I then spend several months writing the book; when I deliver the typescript I get another few hundred pounds — the "on delivery advance". Some months later I receive the "on publication advance". Thereafter, I have to wait until sales of the book have earned more in royalties than the advances already paid, before I get another penny. Total earnings on any one book have never — yet, but I live in hopes — exceeded four figures. And I have a long wait to get up to decent figures.

Conversely, when I put on my one-day lecture course in technical writing I ask a specific fee which, depending on the employer, can be in excess of two hundred pounds a day. By running the one-day course twice during a week, I can get paid as much for two days work as I get for one of the advances on a book. Of course, the initial preparation work on the course material took several days work; but the more often I run the course, the more that expense is spread, and the less important it is.

Payment for lecture courses is usually made within a month. Lecturing pays better than writing, and more quickly. But, of course, I don't lecture every day; not even once every week. Jobs are relatively few. The market is limited. A business plan identifies these facts — in advance.

Suppose that, instead of being a writer, I had been a potter — a maker of mugs. The comparison of profitability — "potting" and lecturing — would then have needed to take account of the capital investment entailed in setting up a potter's workshop. I would need to take account of the cost of the potter's wheel and the kiln. And the clay. And the electricity to run the kiln. And the impact of selling mugs "by the one". And so it goes on.

I'd need to sell a whole lot of mugs to equate with one day's lecturing. I'll stick to my writing and talking.

Let us look at the reasons for a mini-business-person to formulate a business plan. Not all the reasons will apply to every mini-business. But most will. A business plan will help you:

To borrow money: If you are seeking a loan for your mini-business, the bank manager will almost certainly insist on a properly prepared business plan. Even if you have all the capital you need and enough income (a pension perhaps) to provide "eating money" while establishing your operation, you may find that your cash-flow pattern is such that you need an occasional overdraft facility from the bank. You will get this more readily approved if you can show the manager a realistic business plan. And even if you intend to tap Uncle Charles for your capital, he has a right to know what it's all about.

To ensure that your money is wisely invested: Even if you don't need a bank loan, but can set up your mini-business with your own capital, you need to recognise that, by so doing, you are yourself losing interest from eg a building society.

If you don't repay yourself the same interest as the money could earn elsewhere, your mini-business may be costing you money rather than making the required profit. That's a hobby — not a mini-business. (And that's why I always advise beginning writers to defer the purchase of a word-processor until they can pay for it out of writing earnings.)

To assess the market: It would be all too easy to assume that because you can earn, say, £200 for one day's lecturing, you can continue to earn that sort of money week after week. Face it, you can't. A business plan will make you come to terms with realities.

It is also part of the market assessment process to think — in advance, as part of the preparation of the business plan — about how you are going to reach the market. It is pointless setting up shop — selling sandwiches, say — in the middle of Salisbury Plain, if the likely purchasers work in large urban areas. There are only a limited number of opportunities for one-day lecturing; you must contact them all.

Another part of the market assessment process is to ask yourself: not, "What can I make or do, that I can sell?" but rather, "What do the customers/clients out there want, that I can make or do?" And that's a very important difference in emphasis. In business, it is not what you want, but what the customer wants, that counts. At least, it should be.

To keep track of the market: This is an ongoing, post-start-up, advantage of the business plan.

Assessing the market at the start of your endeavours is not enough; you must keep your plan up-to-date. The needs of the market change; if you do not recognise the signs of change, preferably before the tide goes out, you could be left high and dry; you could be trying to sell a product or service which is no longer needed. Yet the change in the needed product or service may only be small. If you identify the forthcoming changes early enough, you will usually be able to adapt to the new requirements.

And of course, if you can get *ahead* of the market, you may be able to make a killing. But be careful. If you get it wrong, you could go bust.

To decide how best to run your mini-business: You may be a real whizz at computer programming and like nothing better than working all day, squinting at the monitor. But if that leaves you no time to get out and *hustle* for more work, you will soon run out of money. Alternatively, you may be a first-class sales-person. But if that takes up too much of your time, and you don't produce the goods or services to sell, the business will not succeed.

The business plan helps you to identify the several aspects of the work that your new mini-business will entail. It will bring home to you the need to allow time (and time equals money) for selling as well as for production — and anything else that has to be done.

To assess the workload: This is a corollary of the previous point. You have to assess the overall size of the business you are getting into.

If you bite off more than you can comfortably chew, you could easily end up with acute indigestion. If you don't meet, eg, the delivery deadlines to which you commit yourself, you could be in considerable financial trouble. A buyer could sue you for non-delivery of a big order. (Delivering all your exquisite Christmas tree decorations on say, 23 December, instead of in mid-November, would not be a good idea.) And, don't forget, as a sole trader, yours is the total financial liability.

And finally the business plan will be of great value in helping you:

To check on your performance: Because the business plan includes a forecast of your cash flow, it is soon apparent if the financial side is going wrong. Remember, more than half the new businesses started each year, fail to make the grade financially. If the money side goes wrong, everything goes wrong.

Having, I hope, successfully explained why a business plan is an essential element in even the smallest and most "service-oriented" of mini-businesses, let us now elaborate on its content. The business plan of a mini-business which does not expect to require outside financial assistance need be only a very simple document. But however simple, it will be of most help if you go through the full discipline, and set it down on paper.

Business objectives

First, the aims and objectives of your mini-business. You have already decided what you are going to do. Write it down as briefly and as unambiguously as you can. It might be something like:

To sell my services as a computer programmer at the highest available market rates.

Or perhaps:

To establish and run a home-based antiques business specialising in Oriental items — other than china and porcelain (ie, excluding breakable items). Sales will be from antique market stalls or from home.

Or, another type of mini-business:

To make and sell, direct to the public and through shops, a range of wrought iron house name-plates.

These three examples are representative of a wide range of mini-business occupations. For computer programmer, read: teacher, lecturer, management or other consultant, writer, solicitor, gardener, cleaning service, etc. For antiques dealer, read any non-productive entrepreneurial activity. For "fancy blacksmith", read: sculptor, painter, cameo-, furniture-or even candlestick-maker, and so on.

The next matters to specify within the "Objectives" section of the business plan are — the decisions we have already made — the intention to trade as an individual, ie as a sole trader, and the intention to remain a one-person operation.

These decisions might be expressed in the form:

The business will operate on a sole trader basis, under my own name, Egbert William Efficiency; while it is intended to be highly efficient and to maximise profits, it is not intended that the business should grow beyond a one-person operation.

Against the possibility that you might need to approach someone else — even Uncle Charles — for financial assistance, it is now worth including a reference to your own abilities. You should outline why your personal services are marketable, ie, your expertise; spell out your experience and/or skills in the selling or in the production of the goods to be sold. Something like:

> *Over the last ten years, since graduating from Muddlecombe University in 1980 with BA (Hons - 2i) Mathematics, I have gained a wide experience in the use of Fortran, Cobol and Basic languages; I have designed and written one-off program suites for use by ABC Ltd, OPQ and Partners, and XYZ (US) Inc. I am a recognised expert on business efficiency programs for the Sinclair Spectrum computer.*

Or, for the antique dealer:

> *I have collected (non-breakable) Oriental antiques, on a personal basis, for the last fifteen years. I am well-known to dealers throughout the South of England as a specialist collector; my advice is frequently sought by dealers on my specialist subjects. For the last five years, I have worked as a buyer for and general assistant to Joan Jones (Antiques) Ltd of Muddlecombe, gaining general trade experience.*

Even if you are unlikely to need financial assistance, the setting down of your objectives and your personal abilities is a useful exercise. It helps to clear the mind. And it might help to boost your mini-business morale if later, it occasionally sags. It probably will.

Market assessment

The next element in the business plan is your assessment of the market — and how you plan to capture part of it.

Market research (and marketing generally) is of considerable importance in any mini-business; it is considered further, in Chapter 5. For now, though, it is sufficient to recognise that a business plan needs an

appraisal of the market. You need to satisfy yourself —
and possible investors (the bank manager or Uncle
Charles) — that your idea is viable.

You need to be able to show that:

- there is a potential demand for your product/service
  — to say that *there ought to be* is not good enough;
- the market is likely to continue — ie, it is neither a
  declining, nor a one-off, demand, nor are your
  abilities likely to be rapidly out-dated; (if a new computer is introduced, could you cope?)
- the market is open to you — someone else may have
  it all sewn up — and maybe you can't break the ties;
- you can compete — successfully — with other suppliers of similar goods or services.

Apply the S-O-P test:

S - Strengths
- *what are the strengths of your position?*
- *in what ways are you (and your product or service) better than the competition?*

O - Opportunities
- *what size is the market?*
- *is it open to you and can you reach it?*

P - Problems
- *what are your (personal) weaknesses?*
- *in what ways are the competition better than you?*
- *what of the future?*

Capital resources and requirements

Depending on the purpose of your mini-business, there
may be no need for any comment under the Capital
Resources heading in your business plan. If your
business is lecturing you probably need no more than

... yourself — and you don't need to pay for that. If your business is writing though, you will need a word processor. (The day of the ordinary "tripewriter" has long passed.) A word processor costs "capital". If you are in the pottery business, you will want a wheel and a kiln and ... These too will require capital. And, sometimes, they will need replacing. In the antiques business, you will need a stock, to trade in. You need capital to buy that stock.

The Capital Resources and Requirements section of your business plan may therefore be a mere "NIL" statement, or it may require some detailing.

If you already own eg your word processor, you should note down what it cost and a pessimistic estimate of what it is now worth. Next, acknowledge that your word processor will not last for ever and that you will need to replace it. Make a note of when that is likely to be, and estimate what the new machine will then cost. Think too, and comment, on how you are going to meet the replacement cost — probably from a depreciation fund. Your equipment is a "capital asset".

If however, you are setting out on a career as an antiques dealer, your "equipment" may be no more than a small folding table. But you will need, "working capital" too — in the form of cash, or a stock of saleable antiques. Your working capital should also be enough to tide you over any delays in your receiving payments due. (Remember too, that your working capital will probably need to increase annually, with inflation.)

If you are VAT-registered (*See* Chapter 10) you should exclude the VAT element from the capital statements; VAT is merely a transfer of money on behalf of Government. If you are not VAT-registered, you will of course, include in the cost statements any VAT you will have to pay.

For our freelance computer programmer then, the

Capital statement in the business plan will look something like this:

Capital Assets
Box-o-Trix PC computer
(purchased 31.2.98, valued at 1.3.00)   £1000.00
(Replacement cost, estimated required at
1.1.03 = £5,000)
Working Capital
Cash in bank   £ 200.00
Required loan   £2000.00

Total assets and capital required   *£3200.00*

For the antique dealer, the Capital statement might look something like this:

Capital assets
Equipment   *Negligible*
Car, current value   £6000.00
Working Capital
Stock   £2000.00
Debtors   £ 500.00
Cash in bank   £1500.00

Total assets and working capital   *£10000.00*

Now let us look at the other financial parts of the business plan; the assessment of your day-to-day operations. First, the profit plan.

The profit plan

The simplest way to prepare a profit plan is to do it month by month — for at least your first year's operations.

Rule up a large (A3) sheet of paper into 14 columns. These will be used for: the names of the items being priced (head the column "Item"), the 12 months of the year, and the annual total. Now divide each of the monthly columns and the annual total column in two; head one "Budget" and the other "Actual".

On the first line of the "Items" column, write "Receipts". Below this list the different types of income you expect: this may just be sales, or it may be lecture fees, or royalties, Public Lending Right, etc. (on books) or it may be all of these. Below all of these, enter "Total receipts" and rule a line across.

Now re-head the remainder of the "Items" column as "Direct Costs". Here, list the items on which you expect to spend money directly related to the receipts. With a one-person mini-business this will usually only be purchase of materials; you will not usually have wages to pay. As before, total these, as "Total direct costs" and rule a line across the sheet.

Next, enter a line-heading: "Gross Profit (Receipts less Direct Costs)". Leave a few lines space — you may feel inclined to calculate the Gross Profit as a percentage of the Total Receipts (Sales) — and again enter a new line-Heading: "Overheads".

Overheads are all the costs that do not relate directly to a product, but are incurred in running the business. It is easy to overlook some overheads; a checklist is therefore useful. You should allow for (and enter line-headings in the "Items" column for):

- rent and rates — that proportion of the total cost that relates to the part of your home used for your mini-business (*See* Chapters 4 and 10)
- lighting and heating — as above
- telephone rental and call charges — as above
- home maintenance, repair and insurance — as above
- any commercial insurance specific to the mini-business
- travel costs not otherwise reimbursed
- stationery and postage (a major item in some mini-businesses)

- advertising costs — all promotional expenses
- legal and other fees associated with the mini-business
- indirect wages — labour costs not directly associated with production (eg part-time secretary, book-keeper, or researcher)
- bank charges and interest on loans
- National Insurance contributions — *see* Chapter 10
- sundries — the inevitable unclassifiable odds and ends.
- depreciation — money set prudently aside to meet the cost of replacement of capital items.

Next, enter a line-heading "Total Overheads"; below that another, "Net Pre-Tax Profit (Gross Profit less Overheads)". And note that, depending on the size of your profit, it will be liable for tax. (*See* Chapter 10.)

So far, the profit plan has been easy, merely writing in headings. Now we come to the difficult, crystal-ball-gazing, bit. You have to insert figures for each of the listed items, in each of the monthly "Budget" columns.

Of course, all the figures can only be estimates, but you should do your best to make them realistic. Be pessimistic in your estimates of receipts and over-generous in your estimating of costs. To do the opposite, and be over-optimistic in your forecasting can only lead to gloom later.

Allow a *monthly* figure for all *costs* — even where the actual expenditure is quarterly (like public utilities) or even annually (like licenses or insurances). This gives you a more realistic picture of the monthly profit. If you are (or expect to be) VAT-registered (*See* Chapter 10), then all figures should exclude the VAT element — it being merely a transfer. If your mini-business is going to be too small to warrant VAT registration you must include the VAT in the costs.

Finally, you must, of course, sum all the columns, sub-columns, and overall totals. It is likely that, at least in the annual totals, your receipts will exceed your direct costs; what is less certain is that you will achieve a *net* profit — ie after allowing for overheads — in the first year. You need to consider the annual totals very carefully indeed.

Figure 2.1 Part of the pre-start-up profit plan for the freelance computer programmer

ITEM	JANUARY BUDGET	JANUARY ACTUAL	FEBRUARY BUDGET	FEBRUARY ACTUAL	MARCH BUDGET	MARCH ACTUAL	ANNUAL TOTAL BUDGET	ANNUAL TOTAL ACTUAL
	£	£	£	£	£	£	£	£
RECEIPTS								
Contract fees	2000		1000*		2000		20000	
Articles	100		50		150		1000	
Total receipts	2100		1050		2150		21000	
DIRECT COSTS								
Nil	0		0		0		0	
Total Direct costs	0		0		0		0	
Gross profit (Receipts - Dir. Costs)	2100		1050		2150		21000	
Gross profit %	100		100		100		100	
OVERHEADS								
Household expenses	100		100		100		1200	
Telephone	50		50		50		600	
Travel	20		20		20		240	
Liability insurance	40		40		40		480	
Agency fees	100		100		200		2000	
Advertising	20		20		20		240	
NIC	20		20		20		240	
Bank charges	20		20		20		240	
Depreciation†	200		200		200		2400	
Sundries	50		50		50		600	
Total Overheads	620		620		720		8240	
Net pre-tax profit	1480		430		1430		12760	

*Holiday
†To meet £5000 replacement cost — *see* Capital statement.

Figure 2.1 shows parts of the profit plan that might be prepared for our computer programmer's mini-business.

The profit plan lets you think again. It lets you reconsider whether your mini-business is actually going to make money. Is it a true mini-business or an expensive self-indulgent hobby?

If the profit plan does show a net loss at the end of the first year, you should review your operational plans. Think about whether you can organise the business differently, more efficiently, less expensively. Do you really need that new equipment? Can you trim down your costs? Can you attract more sales? (Where from? Is this realistic?) Or will things really get better in the second year? If you believe this, demonstrate it, by compiling a second year's profit plan.

Whatever you do though, at this stage, while preparing your detailed profit and loss forecasts:

*** DON'T FOOL YOURSELF ***

Remember — fifty per cent of new small businesses go bust; ie, they fail financially. You can make your own success more likely by making your business plan as realistic and truthful as possible. Get it right *before* you start — not after, as a panic measure.

The cash-flow forecast

Now for another shock. You may already have seen individual months in your profit plan schedule showing a net loss. The actual situation will almost certainly be worse.

In the profit plan you allowed for the big items of expense to be spread throughout the year. In fact, the bills have to be paid at specific times. And to make matters worse, your own earnings will seldom come in as quickly as you anticipate.

Cash-flow problems — that is, the inbalance between when the money actually comes in and when it has to go out — are a major reason for a business getting into serious financial trouble.

To produce a cash-flow forecast you need another large (A3) sheet ruled up exactly the same as for the profit plan — with 14 columns, 13 of which are doubles, headed with the months and "Annual Total" and each sub-headed "Budget" and "actual".

Down the "Item" column you need generally similar line-headings as for the profit plan: Receipts, details of receipts, Total Receipts; next you want a main line-heading "Payments" followed by "Payments for Goods" and then by all the overhead items. At the foot of the "Item" column you then need the following self-explanatory line-headings: "Total Payments"; "Net Cash-flow (Total Receipts less Total Payments)"; "Bank balance at start of month"; "Bank balance at end of month (Balance at start less net cash outflow)".

That was the "easy bit". Now, as before, we come to filling in the figures. you must take all of the figures included in the profit plan and think about when the payments come in and out will actually occur.

In many one-person mini-businesses, the receipts will be largely from cash sales; in such a situation the "cash inflow" should not cause a problem — as long as there is enough of it. But in some mini-businesses some money comes in long after the work is done. Writing is a case in point.

Some years ago, I got an advance of £400 for one of my books: £200 on signing the contract and £200 on publication (about a year later). The first royalties, amounting to £350 over and above the advance, were paid a year after publication; since then, the royalties have been roughly £200 a year. Overall, I am well up into four figures. but it has taken several years to reach that level.

I completed the *work* on that book years ago, within a few months of signing the contract, about nine months before publication. That sort of cash inflow could (but didn't because I was then working only part-time at my mini-business) have landed me with a cash-flow problem.

You need to allow for capital expenditure items in your cash-flow forecast too. They may have a very significant effect on the pattern of the figures at the foot of each column.

Even without capital items, the net cash flow will almost certainly need careful looking at. It is this figure that may well determine whether or not you will need a bank loan or overdraft facility. An overdraft facility will balance out the heavy outgoings with the late incomings. And, remember, if you do need such not-already-allowed-for overdraft/loan facilities, you will have to pay for them — which means adjusting your profit plan.

Figure 2.2 shows part of the cash-flow forecast for the computer programmer's mini-business, as in *Figure 2.1*. The same basic figures are used and can be followed through.

Another major item to be allowed for in the cash-flow forecast is VAT. (For more details on VAT, *see* Chapter 10.) While, in the profit plan, a VAT-registered business should show all receipts and expenditure net of VAT, the VAT must be included in the cash-flow forecast. You will collect VAT in small amounts perhaps; you pay it out in a large — and noticeable —quarterly sum. This will certainly affect your cash-flow position.

There is a further point relating to the financial part of the business plan. Having completed your plan, you may find that, after all, you need a bank loan (or overdraft facility). The bank is unlikely to consider such a request with favour unless there is some personal financial commitment. You need to be able to show that you have invested some capital of your own in your mini-business.

Figure 2.2 Part of the cash-flow forecast for the freelance computer programmer — based on same material as Fig. 2.1.

ITEM	JANUARY BUDGET £	JANUARY ACTUAL £	FEBRUARY BUDGET £	FEBRUARY ACTUAL £	MARCH BUDGET £	MARCH ACTUAL £	ANNUAL TOTAL BUDGET £	ANNUAL TOTAL ACTUAL £
RECEIPTS								
Contract fees*			2000		1000		18000	
Articles*			50		100		900	
Total receipts			2050		1100		18900	
DIRECT COSTS								
Household expenses	100		100		100		1200	
Telephone‡	100						600	
Travel	150						240	
Liability insurance					480		480	
Agency fees*			200		100		1800	
Advertising	120						240	
NIC	20		20		20		240	
Bank charges					60		240	
Depreciation	200		200		200		2400	
Sundries	150		20		10		600	
Income Tax & NIC-4					500		2800	
Total payments	840		540		1470		10840	
Net Cash-flow (Tot rec - Tot pay)	-840		1510		-370		8060	
Bank balance at start month†	200		-640		870		200	
Bank balance at end month (Start bal + cash-flow)	-640		870		500		8260	

*Payments running slightly late, from start-up.
‡Only 3 quarterly statements reflect freelance operations. January account is pre-start-up.
†This is a separate business account. 'Eating money' is available in personal account.

Monitoring

Do not think, when you remove the cold damp towel from your forehead, that once you have finished preparing the business plan, that's it. Having made the plan, and started the business, you must forever *monitor* your performance.

At the end of each month, you should complete the "Actual" columns in the profit plan and the cash-flow forecast sheets. Now, the figures are facts; not the product of a steamed-up, rosy-red crystal ball. You must check — carefully and regularly — to see how the actual figures vary from the ones in the "Budget" column.

Where there are variations — and there will be many — you must find out *why*. Did you forget an overhead item? Amend the "Budget" figures to include it. Are payments coming in even slower than you anticipated? Can you do anything to expedite them? Maybe you can issue your bills or invoices a day or so earlier and get into the purchaser's earlier payment batch. Why have you spent so much on stock? Are you now overstocked . . . or have sales varied accordingly? Or have sales just not come up to expectations? How can you boost your sales?

Each month initially, and perhaps less frequently later, you need to watch your finances carefully. If the money goes wrong, the business goes bust. Your business plan is the best tool you can have, to ensure that your mini-business is successful. Use it.

CASE STUDY *Joy and George*

Joy and George are husband and wife, both now retired. For several years they have each run their own separate art/craft mini-businesses. They operate as individual "sole traders". Joy is a miniaturist — painting miniature pendants and brooches; George makes a wide variety of turned wooden objects for household use or ornament (knife-handles, candlesticks, etc.)

Both Joy and George started up their skill-based mini-businesses from scratch in their sixties, when they retired; both look on their activities as agreeable and profitable hobbies — no more than a pleasant way of supplementing their pensions.

Joy had been a leisure painter all her adult life and only took up miniature painting when she retired. She now works at home (but with no "special" room) most afternoons, painting her miniatures. Her start-up expenses were small — materials, etc. — requiring no outside financial assistance. It took Joy some while to become adept at the new skills required for her miniatures, but she considers she is now successful — in relation to the amount of time she puts in.

She sells her work mainly through galleries and exhibitions but also works on commissions obtained from personal recommendations. She maintains an album of colour photographs of her work which she can show to potential clients.

Her mini-business does not earn a lot — but this is acceptable, it being only a pension supplement. Anyway, "It is an unusual artist who earns much," says Joy. Despite the small income (and remember, she doesn't work anything like full time at it), Joy would happily do the same thing again; she thoroughly enjoys her lot.

A spare-time writer, too, she has had several articles published about miniature painting — generating spin-off publicity for her own work. She is now contemplating a book about contemporary miniaturists.

George retired and started up his mini-business rather earlier than Joy; initially he was much busier than he is now. George puts this down to a general over-crowding in the craft field. He works from home, with a workshop in the garden; this is fitted out with a limited amount of specialist equipment —lathe, band-saw, etc — for the purchase of which he required no financial assistance.

Nowadays, George makes only a small profit from his mini-business; but like Joy's, it is looked on as a pension supplement rather than a source of income. He sells his work largely from stalls at occasional craft fairs and markets but has also supplied local shops on a sale or return basis.

He advises those about to start a mini-business to research their market thoroughly.

Joy and George are good examples of retired people running small but reasonably successful mini-businesses — as profitable hobbies. Neither felt the need to produce a business plan before they started. But hobby or no, they are business-like in their activities.

3
YOU – THE PRIME MOVER

Time is a *scarce resource*. So is money. But time is scarcer than money. You can always borrow money, but no one can squeeze more than 24 hours out of any one day. That is a truism. And nowhere is it more true than in a one-person mini-business.

Another comment, equally relevant in any business, is the famous one of C Northcote Parkinson, that: "Work expands so as to fill the time available for its completion." These two basic concepts are in conflict — particularly in a mini-business.

Think back to how it is for a wage-slave. If a wage-slave stops and chats to a colleague, or idles away the time on unproductive work, the boss probably doesn't like it. But what is the boss to do? An employee is difficult to dismiss — if the grounds are in any way dubious, the employer can be called before an Industrial Tribunal. Even if the employee is "safely" dismissed, it is time-consuming and costly to train a replacement. So . . . as long as the wage-slave doesn't waste too much time, his/her job is reasonably secure, and the pay cheque comes through at the end of each month.

In a one-person mini-business the situation is very different. It can be summed up as:

** NO WORK = NO OUTPUT = NO PAY **

So . . . in a mini-business you must keep at it. You can't afford "make-weight" activities. There will be so much truly productive work that has to be done, that there will often not be enough hours in the day.

Above all therefore, you — the prime mover in the mini-business — must use your time wisely. You must plan how to make the best use of it. Do that by:

- considering the relationship between work and family and segregating work from leisure
- planning ahead — using diaries, charts, lists, etc.
- determining priorities and setting yourself targets.

Family relationships

First, the family. No mini-business can be a success if the rest of the family opposes it. If your spouse has been looking forward to your retirement as a time for greater togetherness, an out-of-the-blue proposal for a full-time mini-business is unlikely to get an ecstatic welcome.

If you are a woman and propose to establish a mini-business, your husband (and children too perhaps) will immediately start worrying about food. If you are working, who is going to get the dinner? He will not be wildly enthusiastic about a flippant suggestion that he can cook his own. This is not sexist, it's an inevitable and instinctive reaction. At the very least, you should broach the idea delicately and tentatively, over a period of time. You never know, he might learn to like cooking.

To make your mini-business a real success, you should make allowances for the — both real, and perceived — needs of the rest of the family in making your own plans. Don't start off with a conflict of interests. The would-be working wife could perhaps budget for eating out more often, for hiring a house-cleaner and for sending washing to the laundry. Equally, the early-retired man who wants to spend all hours at his mini-business could perhaps make provision for employing a gardener.

Plan on a 6-hour — rather than an 8-hour — day, perhaps. Or maybe setting aside one day each week for "togetherness" could be the right answer. (Reinstate the weekend — which will otherwise disappear.)

For the younger mini-business-person though, without the cushion of a pension or working partner, the operation must be a full-time job. It has to be worked at every day, from 9 to 5. (Initially at least, the hours will probably work out far longer.) The mini-business cannot be treated as something to be played at, or worked at half-heartedly.

Discuss your mini-business with your family. Agree the hours you will work — and then stick to them as best you can. You can almost certainly put in extra time when it doesn't conflict with family requirements. You can always work nights. It may help if you can involve the family in the business; children can sometimes be encouraged to answer the phone — so long as they can take sensible messages — and enjoy it. Especially once they realise that your mini-business is paying for their next holiday or new bike.

As part of the family agreement, there should also be a *quid pro quo* — in your favour. The family should agree that they will not interrupt you during your working hours for anything short of a national disaster. (And that would not include a social call by the vicar. If you were working away from home the family would have to cope with him on their own. Let them do so again.)

The family should also be persuaded to recognise that, for a few months when you are starting up the new mini-business, you will have to work extra hard, for extra long hours. You will be able to make up for this later by having more money to play with.

Once the mini-business is up and running though, remember that all work and no play makes Jack or Jill a dull person. You MUST take time off from your mini-business. Once established, stick to your agreed work-schedule.

Planning your time

The business up and running, you can plan the use of your time. The days of frantic hustling and panic working are . . . well, not gone, but at least less frantic, and no longer continuous. Now, you can consciously decide which task you will do when. And there are several common-place tools for planning:

- diaries — including the much-mocked "organisers"
- wall — and other, charts
- lists — things to do, things to order, things to get, things to fix, things to arrange, people to meet, and so on.

Diaries first. Every business-person needs one — and probably has to live with two or three. And that's when the trouble starts. You keep a small diary in your pocket or handbag; you probably have another diary on your desk; and your spouse will probably keep another. Without a lot of care, the three diaries quickly get "out of kilter". This is particularly important when your mini-business involves the selling of your personal services.

You visit a client who offers you some work; you look in your pocket diary and agree to do a day's "out-work" on the 23rd. You get back to your home-office and make a quick note in the main office diary. Meanwhile, your partner checks his/her diary, sees you are free that day, and arranges for friends to visit. Result: a minor family problem — but you should not sacrifice the work.

This problem can be even more difficult when, even though all diaries are up-to-date and identical, two work bookings are made for the same day. You are away from home and agree a date; your partner takes a phone call in your absence and agrees another job on the same date. This can easily happen. But it can happen as easily to a high-powered wage-slave as to a mini-businessperson. Businesses will therefore understand about double-booking — so long as you re-schedule quickly.

As soon as you discover you are double-booked, telephone one of the clients and re-schedule. (Think which client pays the most and reschedule the other; or ask the clients with whom you are on the best terms, if they will re-schedule. A good relationship will usually weather an occasional re-scheduling.)

Use your diary too, to plan your own work programme. Reserve time for your own purposes: time to do the accounts, time to order more material, time to work — even time off.

It is an unfortunate fact that, left to our own devices, we all prefer to waste time. We invent things that have to be done, before we start what we should really be doing. (And writers are some of the worst offenders in this respect. Almost anything seems preferable to starting on that empty page. Replying to unproductive letters is my favourite "cop-out".)

In big business, management consultants are often called in — to improve efficiency. One of their standard ploys is to ask such clients to keep a *time log*. That is, a detailed record, by quarter-hour sections, of how each person's work-time is spent. Having logged the activities, the clients are invited to classify the importance of each quarter-hour occupation.

It is worth applying the same discipline to your own mini-business. The usual result — in businesses big or small — is a discovery that far too much time is being spent on unimportant and irrelevant tasks. We will look at this result in more detail in the next section — on priorities and personal targets. For now, accept that it is worth spending time planning, in your "organiser diary" perhaps, how to best use your limited time.

Another aspect of the planning process which is often recommended — and which is equally relevant to the one-person mini-business — is the time-chart. The time-chart comes most into its own when your mini-business is about largish single projects — producing paintings, books, computer programs, etc. In my own business of writing non-fiction books I find it particularly useful.

How is it useful? It is no good getting a contract or commission to produce a book (or work of art, or program) and then just working at it, without thought of tomorrow. If you are "in business" you need an on-going supply of projects and commissions. So you need to start seeking the next commission well before you have finished the one in hand. To do that needs planning.

This — what I am now writing — is the third chapter of this present book. I expect to complete the book within three or four more months: all the planning and most of the research has already been done; only the writing remains. (Only?) I already have a contract for the next book — to be delivered about eight months from now. I have a proposal, complete with sample chapter, for another book being seriously considered; and two more book proposals which are at a more tentative stage.

I know — subject to unforseen circumstances — that I can cope with this workload; this confidence is partly because I have scheduled the work on a time-chart. *Figure 3.1* shows my tentative work schedule as it is at the moment — half way through Chapter 3. In reality, the progress will vary, but planning it out like this reassures me that I should be able to cope. I shall re-schedule the chart from time to time, as existing work nears completion and other projects are commissioned. Or rejected.

Whatever the basis of your mini-business the same planning principles can readily be applied to your work. The antique dealer might wish to chart the dates of important antique fairs, for which a good stock has to

Figure 3.1 A typical schedule of work in hand, based on the author's situation at Chapter 3 in the present book. Similar work schedules could be developed for other activities.

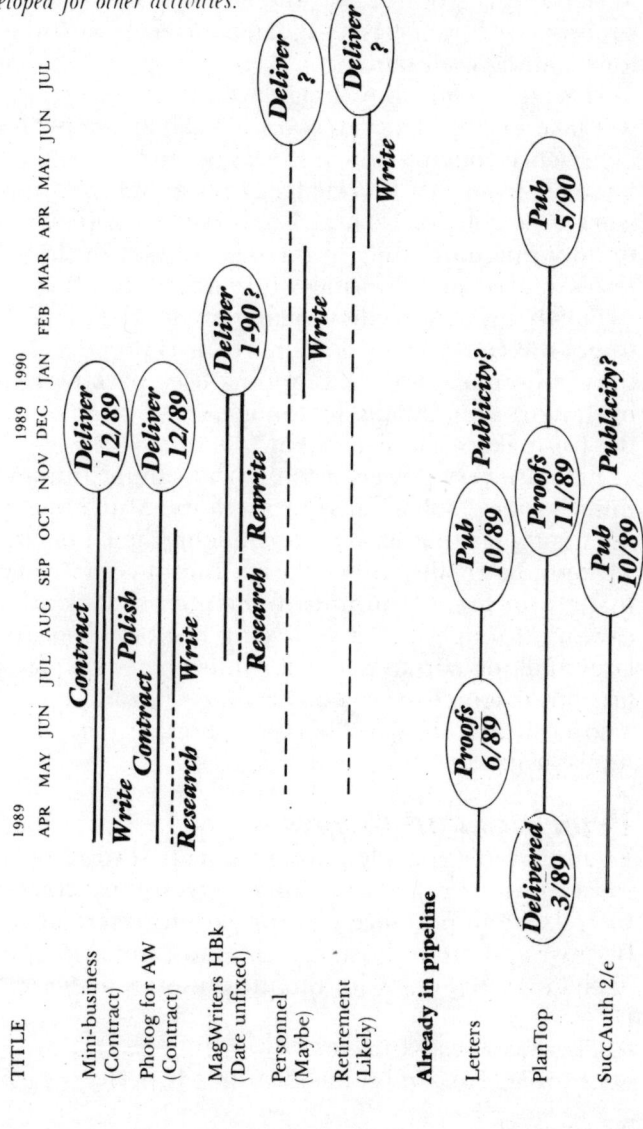

be built up. The fancy blacksmith might win a contract for name plates for a whole new housing estate, or wish to build up a stock of saleable items — fancy light-supports or flower-basket-hangers perhaps — for a forthcoming craft fair.

How do I know how long each of my own projects will take to complete? In two ways. First, I know from experience roughly how fast I work; and secondly because, from that knowledge, I set myself a realistic work timetable for each project. I will explain my work programme more fully in the next section of this chapter — under the "Priorities and targets" heading.

Finally though, while thinking about planning, don't forget the common or garden list. It is popular to mock those who make lists — shopping lists, packing lists, lists of things to do, people to contact, etc. But don't mock the list-makers: emulate them.

Lists are very powerful tools. You cannot run a whole mini-business solely on your memory. Much better to list the things that have to be bought, the letters to be written, the replies to be chased. But of course, having made your list — you must remember to look at it, and to work through it. Get yourself a peg-board, or fix a large bulldog clip to the wall some where. Display your list; put it somewhere you can't miss it, can't ignore it. And keep it up to date. It's an important part of your mini-business.

Priorities and targets

Finally, in this consideration of how best to use your most precious resource — time — you must think about the relative importance of your various tasks. And because you are in business, the most important task is likely to be the one with the most money associated with it.

There is a well-known law in business, known as the 80/20 rule. For a mini-business this is perhaps best expressed as: eighty per cent of the profit comes from twenty per cent of the effort; conversely, the other eighty per cent of the effort generates no more than twenty per cent of the profits. (The 80/20 concept seems to apply with equal relevance to a wide variety of business situations.) The prime task of any business-person is, of course, to identify the profitable "twenty per cent effort" tasks, and direct more of the less productive effort towards these. Think about it.

But important though the money side undoubtedly is, completion dates are more so. Delivery dates must be sacrosanct. If you have agreed to deliver something by a specific date, you MUST meet that deadline. Mini-businesses that miss delivery dates often miss future contracts too.

Your business plan too — no matter how simplistic it was — will have been based on a target level of output. If you fail to maintain the planned level of output, your estimates of profit too, will not be met. (And there is usually some element of "gearing" in the profit forecasts — a small fall-off in output or deliveries can easily lead to a much more significant fall in profits.)

So . . . it is helpful to sort out the more important tasks from the less important; it is essential to work to forecast deadlines. And in order to be sure that you are doing this, you should *monitor* your progress.

My own working methods are to set myself deadlines for each element of a job. I set these internal deadlines against a known — or, if necessary, self-imposed — overall deadline for a complete project.

Figure 3.2 shows the actual timetable to which I am trying to work in writing this book. It allows, realistically I hope, for the weeks when I have outside commitments that reduce my writing output. And I monitor my progress against that timetable every weekend. From this timetable, I *know* — inasmuch as anything is that certain — that I shall meet my contracted delivery date. (And

Figure 3.2. The work-timetable (as at Chapter 3 stage) for this book, and the monitored output to date.

MINI-BUSINESS   Foulshams
Contracted delivery 31 Dec 89

Chap	Target words	Achieved words	Target Run Tot	Achieved Run Tot	Target date	Achieved end-date
1	3000	3500	3000	3500	23/4	23/4
2	5000	5500	8000	9000	14/5	28/4
3	3000	3000	11000	12000	21/5	12/5
4	5000		16000		28/5	
5	4000		20000		11/6	
6	4000		24000		25/6	
7	4000		28000		2/7	
8	3000		31000		9/7	
9	4000		35000		16/7	
10	5000		40000		23/7	

Figure 3.2 continued.

OUTPUT

Week ending date (Sun)	*Target words*	*Achieved words*	*Run total*
23/4	3000	3500	3500
30/4	4000	7500	11000
7/5	—	—	11000
14/5	1000		
21/5	2000		
28/5	4000		
4/6	2000		
11/6	2000		
18/6	2000		
25/6	4000		
2/7	4000		
9/7	4000		
16/7	4000		
23/7	4000		

(Based on 4000 words/week reduced for known non-writing days)

the estimated completion dates derived in *Figure 3.2* have already been reflected in the overall planning included in the earlier *Figure 3.1*.

Figure 3.2 is about a non-fiction, "technical", writing project. (And, to forestall any criticism from my writing friends, I acknowledge that it may be easier for a non-fiction writer to work in this way than it is for a "creative" novelist.) But the approach is equally relevant to many other typical mini-business projects.

A sales-oriented mini-business might — indeed, *should* — set targets and deadlines for volumes of sales and/or for financial returns. A "manufacturing" mini-business could undoubtedly set targets for production figures — one wrought-iron name-plate per day perhaps.

Remember though, all the timetables and targets in the world are of no use if the actual output is not monitored — and compared with the targets — and the timetables themselves amended as circumstances change.

Always plan pessimistically; always set low(ish) targets. Everything always takes longer than you expect it to. Low targets mean safe deadlines, assured delivery dates — and a warm glow of personal satisfaction at having beaten the target. But, at the other extreme, don't set your targets ridiculously low, or the whole process will be valueless.

Being your own boss

Finally, to ensure that you make the best possible use of your time, you must motivate yourself. Not just overall — that's done. You need to motivate yourself specifically for the next hour or so too. As a mini-business-person you no longer have a boss hovering over you to ensure that you work. You are your own boss.

Your motivation now is no longer to avoid the possibility of a "rocket" from the boss; it is more to avoid the stigma of a business failure. Working for yourself, you have all the disadvantages: loneliness; the lack of companionship and the associated lack of scope for consulting colleagues; and the possibility of taking time off without outside criticism. You must guard against these problems.

Don't just set yourself output targets for the week; set yourself smaller tasks and sub-tasks to accomplish within parts of the working day. And reward yourself for accomplishing them. These rewards can be as simple as "No coffee until I've finished these letters," or "If I can get three name-plates made before lunchtime, we'll eat at the pub." ("If not, it's just bread and cheese.")

Home-workers often find it hard to get started each day: they're all right when they get going, but find it difficult to overcome their initial inertia. Most writers — including, in this instance, all those who put pen to paper, not just "proper writers" — seem to suffer from this problem.

I find that reading carefully through the previous day's output, improving it here and cutting it there, helps me to start. I switch on the machine and make the corrections; by doing this relatively easy task, I find I am almost instantly back "in the swing" of writing. Failing that, it often helps to write just anything — even if it has to be scrapped later.

And the same process — of polishing up yesterday's work — will work equally well with other activities too: computer programming, painting, report writing, designing, knitting or . . . The new work will follow on smoothly from the revision of the previous day's work.

4
PREMISES AND EQUIPMENT

This book is about running a mini-business — and the title implies that the business is to be run from home. But that is perhaps taking too narrow a view of the matter.

In most cases, the most sensible place for a home mini-business is just that — home. In a few instances though, it may be better — or even necessary — for the business to be undertaken from other premises. Planning consent may be needed (see below) — and not forthcoming; your home may not have the space you need. And even if you are able to work from home, you need to think about how best to arrange accommodation. That is what the first part of this chapter is about.

Planning considerations

First, you must think about your activity — and its effect on others. Will your mini-business generate unusual noise? (A piece of mechanical equipment to be installed in the garage perhaps?) Will the neighbours object? To preserve friendly relationships, they may put up with the noise when you are only working the odd hour or so a week at your hobby. Their attitudes can change rapidly if a hobby becomes a full-time occupation. A full-time nuisance is never acceptable.

Business visitors to your house can lead to an excess of cars — and even worse, commercial vehicles delivering and collecting goods — parked in a quiet residential road. Your neighbours will soon object to this.

A writer, pounding quietly away at a computer keyboard, or a commercial artist, working at a drawing board, is unlikely to upset anyone. But a musician or a composer could easily become a considerable nuisance.

But it is not merely the neighbours that you need to consider. There are planning laws and regulations about what you can do at or from home. You are *unlikely* to need planning permission so long as:

- you make no more than minor alterations within your house which are not visible from outside;
- the character and use of the building remains essentially residential — ie if you merely use one room as an office or occasional work-room;
- it does not generate an amount of traffic or even just people calling, that would be considered unusual in a residential road;
- you do not disturb the neighbours by making an unreasonable noise or smell;
- you restrict any outward display of your business activities to a discreet name-plate or similar.

If however, you wish to physically extend your house in order to accommodate your business, or propose to construct, for instance, a hard-standing for visiting vehicles, you will need to seek planning permission.

(There is a very helpful booklet about planning requirements, called *A Step by Step Guide to Planning Permission for Small Businesses*, which is published by the Department of the Environment. The Planning Department of your local District Council should be able to provide you with a free copy.

As well as the planning consents that may be required, you will need to check the deeds of your own house or the conditions on the use to which the property may be put. If you are doing anything more than sitting in a room writing, drawing or telephoning, you will be wise to investigate such conditions. It will almost always pay to consult a solicitor too.

It may turn out that your mini-business cannot be run from your home; it may have to be run from shop premises — or even a room over a shop. This added expense will almost certainly entail a revision of your business plan.

Planning and other legal aspects apart, you should at least consider the various accommodation options open to you. You might just find that you will be able to run your mini-business better, if you establish it away from home. Usually though, home's best.

Accommodation options

Depending on your financial resources, and the activity or purpose of your mini-business, the possibilities for its accomodation are, broadly:

- a corner of a room in the house,
- a whole "dedicated" room (a study or . . .),
- a shed in the garden — or the garage,
- a rented room, shop or workshop in a nearby commercial or industrial area, or
- a purpose-built house-cum-workshop/studio.

If your mini-business is to produce and market pottery mugs, you cannot do this from the proverbial cupboard under the stairs. Similarly, an antiques dealer — even a small one — needs adequate storage space; and once again, a mere "corner" is unlikely to suffice. A space-constrained writer, telephone salesperson, computer programmer, or management consultant however, could — with care — establish a very reasonable office "under the stairs".

Figure 4.1 suggests ways of arranging a small, but workable, mini-business office in a mini-space.

Figure 4.1. How to make the most use of minimum space — for a mini-business office.

Using the under-stairs cupboard or other cubbyhole:

- Remove doors or any other obstructions to the use of the full width of the cupboard —replace with curtains or other movable screens to protec the "office" when not occupied.

- Plan carefully, in advance, how you are going to use the space most effectively.

- Use every available inch of wall space for either shelves, peg-boards, or other storage (maybe fix the telephone on the wall too).

- Provide extra, concentrated, lighting on the work-space — but don't waste shelf/desk-top space — clamp a spring-balanced angled lamp to a shelf-edge.

- Remember to provide for more-than-sufficient electric power-points — there will always be another piece of essential equipment.

- Make a work-desk of an extra-wide shelf — fix it at the right height to accommodate eg, filing cabinets beneath it.

- Provide eg, two-drawer height filing cabinets, on wheels, to occupy the knee-space when not in use — spread them ergonomically around you when working.

- Always be tidy.

Figure 4.1 continued.

Using part of the living or dining-room — part time:

- Ideally — don't.

If there is no alternative — for it will often lead to domestic friction — consider the use of one of the "foldaway" expanding bureaux such as:

- **The Home Office:** a modern, wheeled, cupboard-like unit which opens up to twice its width providing space for a typewriter, shelving, filing, etc. Marketed by Scandinavian World, 72-94 Park Road, Crouch End, London N8 8JP.

- **The "King" Private Office:** various arrrangements of bookshelves with roll-out bureaux etc., and extra work-space, all to match the other furniture in a room. Marketed by King Office Furniture Systems, 19-30 Alfred Place, London WC1E 7EA.

Using the attic:

- Never forget the possibility of the attic as a permanent office space for a home mini-business. Spiral stairs can be fitted into the minimum of space; the attic can be floored and windows fitted. There are many firms offering such Loft Conversions. Investigate.

Ideally though, "even" a writer — and all broadly similar activities — will be best served by the use of a whole room which can be fitted out with bookshelves, filing cabinets, and all the now-necessary electrical equipment. In a small way of business, an antiques dealer too, would be content with a single room.

A potter, a glass engraver or a carpenter however would not be welcome within the average domestic household; such craft activities would almost certainly be banished to a workshop.

The shed in the garden or the back part of the garage now comes into it's own. But think about making the garden shed a brick, rather than a flimsy wooden, structure; garden sheds can be very cold in winter; your mini-business is no longer a mere fine weather hobby. You will need to get out there and work — every day, come snow, rain or shine. Certainly the idea of sitting out in a wooden summer-house and pounding my computer keyboard holds no appeal at all, for me —even on a fine Spring day.

If it does look as though you will have to work in a wooden shed, quickly investigate the practicalities of a cordless telephone and connecting up to the electricity supply. No mini-business these days can afford to be without these twin attributes of civilisation. Investigate room-heaters too.

Your mini-business may well be such that you have to work from lock-up premises in a non-residential back — or even High — street. As above, you may be driven to this for planning or other legal reasons. The biggest problem with such a solution is of course the cost. A mini-business may not be able to afford a financial millstone. Your business plan will help you decide about this.

The other major disadvantage of "away-from-home" premises is just that — they are away from home, and all the benefits of home working. Working at home, if you stop work and a client rings, you can be back on the job within seconds; with a High Street office, once you leave for home, you are un-reachable. You may lose an order.

The last of our identified options for mini-business premises entails far more upheaval than any of the others. It is also an option seldom appropriate for other than the "heavier" crafts. This is to buy a whole new (new-to-you) house within which is, or can be, incorporated a workshop or studio and perhaps a sale-room too.

From time to time, new developments of so-called "craft villages" are advertised. Within just a few months prior to the time of writing I have seen advertisements for the non-profit-making Merthyr Craft Village, (Write to Merthyr Tydfil Housing Association, Freepost, Merthyr Tydfil, Mid Glamorgan or phone Peter Davies on 0685 83311.) and the Chaddlewood Farm Studios in Plympton, Devon. (Write to Paul Rose at Ellis & Co., 17 Highfield Road, London NW11 9PJ or phone the Sales Centre at 0752 343025.)

I hold no brief for either development but on paper both look interesting. Both are relatively small — 14 and 23 units respectively — and both offer workshop/studio spaces of up to around 500 square feet plus associated living accommodation. The Merthyr development offers both rented and freehold accommodation and separate workshops; the Plympton development offers freehold combined properties.

There is also always the possibility of buying an existing home/workshop establishment. One-off properties of this type can be found all over the country. Or you can do your own conversion — but watch out for planning permission. Get it all approved before you buy.

If you do buy or convert your own home/workshop, remember that your product will need to be little short of spectacular for the world to beat a path to a too remote door. Your atelier must not be too far from the beaten track; it must be accessible to buyers.

Specific equipment

Having considered the premises — and probably resolved, very sensibly, to do everything in your power to stay put — let us think about equipment. First, equipment specific to your own mini-business activity.

Is your mini-business a wholly new activity, or one that you have already been doing, in your spare time?

If it is a business developed from a past hobby, you probably have much of the necessary equipment already. There is therefore no problem. If you are planning now, well in advance of retirement, to set up a mini-business once you are released from wage-slavery, this too presents a few problems. Indeed, starting up and learning the trade or craft in your spare time, before retirement, is perhaps the ideal way of establishing a mini-business. If nothing else, you can spread the purchases of equipment over a longer period and have your regular ongoing income to cushion you against the costs. (As we recognised in Chapter 1.)

If you are starting completely from scratch though, and raring to go, you have got to meet the full cost of the necessary equipment. Time spent in comparing different types of expensive specialist equipment will never be wasted. Ask around among others in the same line of business; every item of specialist equipment has its own idiosyncrasies — some may be unacceptable *to you*. Look before you leap. It is usually wise to buy the best you can afford; and it is often worth investigating the purchase of second-hand equipment.

Remember too to allow for the purchase of your specialist equipment in your business plan. Murphy's Law says that specialist equipment is always more expensive than you have allowed for. Check out too, whether your equipment can be leased. Leasing can do wonders for your cash flow.

Office equipment

Apart from the specialist equipment needs of your mini-business, you will certainly need some basic office equipment — even if no more than minimal. Whatever your activity, you will need a desk and chair; you will need to write letters and answer telephones; and you will need to keep records.

In many fields of mini-business activity, "office equipment" will be all that is required. Not just "proper writers", but insurance brokers, translators, PR people, computer programmers and analysts, management consultants, and the whole range of office services mini-businesses; all these revolve around the use of basic office equipment.

Let us start by considering the really basic needs of any mini-business. To run a mini-business effectively, you must *communicate* with your customers/clients: you need to write sales and other letters; you need to send out invoices (and reminders); you need to order materials — by phone and/or in writing; and you need to receive orders for work.

The basic minimum equipment for any mini-business is therefore:

- a typewriter (or better — see below) — hand-written communication is just not businesslike;
- a telephone — and ideally, but not essentially, a "work" number which differs from your home number;
- files — and a system by which they are organised.

And of course, this basic equipment needs to have something on which to sit — as do you. So, a minimum of a table, or a desk, or even just a wide shelf, and a chair — ideally a swivel one.

Taking these basic items in turn, first the typewriter. Do not, on any account, fool yourself that you can manage without one. The absolute minimum is a manual semi-portable — and these need cost no more than about £40. (Don't get one that is too light or portable, it won't stand up to the hammering it will inevitably get.) Or — and probably better — you should be able to get a good, solid, second-hand *reconditioned* office machine for about the same price.

But unless you are a practiced typist, a manual typewriter will show up your lack of skill: variations in key pressure from different fingers mean variations in the boldness of different characters, as they appear on the finished page. An electric or electronic typewriter will hide this lack of skill. All characters are *automatically* struck with equal pressures.

(An electric typewriter uses an electric motor to operate conventional type levers. An electronic typewriter uses either: a small hammer hitting character-embossed arms projecting from a fast-spinning wheel —a daisy-wheel; or a number of tiny pins marking the paper in a character-forming pattern of dots — a dot matrix.)

Small electronic typewriters can now be obtained for little more than £100. They will suffice for very light use. If you will need to do much "communicating" in your mini-business though, a heavier electronic typewriter should be considered — at perhaps £300. And once you get up into this price bracket, it is wise to consider the alternative — a budget word processor (see below).

Next the telephone. First, you've got to have one. Secondly, it is almost essential to accompany the telephone with an answering machine.

There are a variety of telephones now available. Think carefully before buying a new phone. The attractive new one-piece instruments may not be the best for office use:

- The one-piece handset will be heavier than a two-piece instrument — and you may have to hold it to

your ear for many long calls.
- a one-piece instrument could accidentally become "engaged" — for instance, if set down askew on a wad of papers — thereby missing business calls. The "call-ended" state is more positive with a two-piece phone.

Answering machines too have proliferated. You need not splurge on an expensive remote control answering machine: one that will simply play back messages on your return to the office will usually suffice, unless your mini-business is very high-powered.

Files may seem mundane and too small to be worth considering — but this attitude can be fatal. A mini-business without records, without files, will almost certainly fail. You need to *know* the state of your mini-business. You need to be able to refer back to letters — your own and those addressed to you. I recommend the use of large lever-arch files. You will need several. We will look later at just how best to organise their use (*See* page 87).

And the last of the fundamentals of your office are the desk and chair. For anything beyond the minimum space, go for a large table-like desk and a basic office swivel and wheeled chair, with arms. Within reason, the bigger the desk-space the better. (My own large work-desk is permanently congested with several piles of "essential" papers.)

If your mini-business entails a lot of sedentary desk-work, you may find you get back pain. To avoid this, it is worth exploring the benefits of a "kneeling chair".

These chairs have pronounced forward-slanting seats, pads to support the knees — and no arm or back rests. The best-known such chairs are in the "Balans" range — but they are not cheap (a minimum of around £200). A much cheaper alternative is a chair designed on similar principles and sold by the mail-order firm of

Scotcade for just under £50. But remember that, at least in terms of durability and sturdiness, you generally get what you pay for. (contact The Back Shop, 24 New Cavendish Street, London W1M 7LH for the "Balans" range and Scotcade, at 33-34 High Street, Bridgnorth, Shropshire WV16 4YT for the less expensive version.)

But let us now explore the equipping of an office for a mini-business which needs more than the minimum. An office for a writer, a PR freelance, a consultant, etc. If your mini-business in any way revolves around "words on paper", you will need more than just the basics. (And increasingly, words are not merely "on paper" —they are often preserved and/or delivered electronically. As we shall see.)

The major expansion of the fundamental office equipment is the word processor and/or the personal computer — the PC.

The office computer

Any word-oriented mini-business — and many other mini-businesses too — can, in these final days of the twentieth century, benefit from using a computer. No, that is insufficiently positive. They cannot do without.

(A typewriter is fine initially, but you should soon be able to financially justify the purchase of a word processor. A good rule of thumb is to buy one just as soon as you can possibly afford it *out of earnings*.)

Before mentioning the inevitable, ubiquitous and much beloved "Amstrad" — the Amstrad PCW 8256/8512/9512 — let us first consider personal computers generally, and in principle.

Far too many people are put off by the apparent complexities of a word processor or personal computer. They need not be. Any computer set up for word processing — for a mini-business, usually the first basic use of the equipment — consists of:

- a keyboard — much like the front half of an old-fashioned typewriter;
- a monitor — a box with a screen, just like a TV, on which the words appear;
- the computer itself — the central processing unit — which also usually incorporates . . .
- one or more disk drives, which have much in common, both in principle and purpose, with audio tape recorders;
- a printer — effectively the "back half" of an electronic typewriter, ie, without the keyboard;
- the word processor program — held on a disk which, when read, via the disk drive, tells the computer what to do.

In simplistic terms, the computer itself, the "box of electronic tricks", consists of a central processor and a memory. The central processor accepts instructions and processes information — receiving it from and sending it to a variety of destinations.

Figure 4.2 illustrates the basic principles of the modern personal computer.

Within the computer itself, the main "destination" is the memory — the *random access memory*, known as RAM. The RAM can be thought of as a bank of electronic switches, which operate as pigeon-holes. Each pigeon-hole holds a tiny piece of information — the switch is either "on" or "off". Many current personal computers (PCs), have a RAM capable of holding 640,000 *bytes* of information. (A memory of this size is referred to as a 640K RAM — the K standing for Kilobyte, approximately 1000 bytes.) Each byte consists of 8 *bits* and each bit is represented by an "on" or "off" state of the switch.

Having read that, forget all about "bits" and how they are stored. It is sufficient to remember that each *byte* represents one character — a number or a letter. A

Figure 4.2 The basic principles and elements of a personal computer (PC) used, in this case, as a word processor.

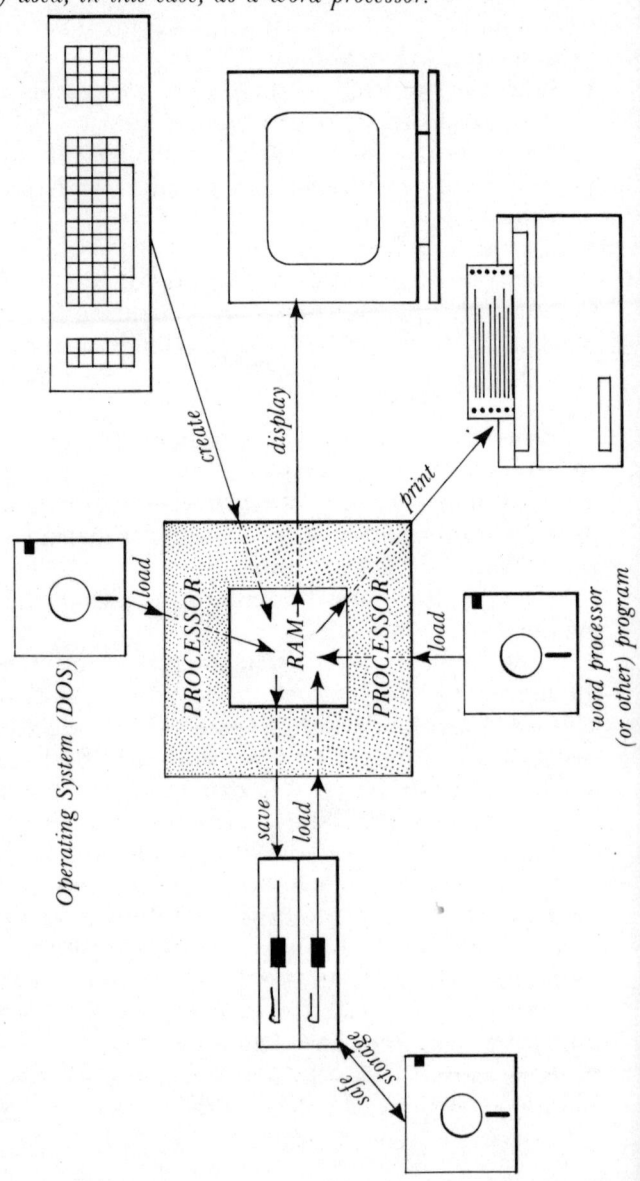

640K RAM therefore will hold 640,000 characters — say 70,000 words, if that were all it contained.

The RAM is effective only when the computer is switched on. The moment the power supply ceases, the memory fails. When using a computer therefore, it is essential to "save" — ie, record on a computer disk — any work in progress or required to be kept. At some future time, it is then possible to read the recorded material back into the RAM and continue to work on it.

But I have jumped ahead. The computer will not do this without its own instructions. It needs to have the operating system (eg "MS-DOS" or "PC-DOS" for a PC) fed into it — ie, "loaded". Every computer has an operating system; smaller, hobby, computers often have it built in; most PCs require the operating system to be loaded at the start of each working session.

Similarly, for a computer to work as a word processor, it needs to have the word processor program loaded into it.

Word processing

Now let us revert to "the Amstrad" — the word processing machine that changed the mini-business world. Until "the Amstrad" was introduced, many professional writers swore by their favourite typewriter — or even that they needed to "feel the words running down their arms to their pen or pencil". Others, myself included, bought relatively cheap "home" computers, struggled to link up all the pieces, and put up with some inconvenience of use. Now though, there is hardly a writer without his or her Amstrad — or better.

What Alan Sugar, the boss of Amstrad did, in late 1985, was to offer a complete, purpose-made, word-processing equipment package, short only of the three-pin mains plug. The computer itself was far from "state of the art" — and therefore of little interest to computer "buffs" — but it did exactly what many people wanted.

It was effectively a replacement typewriter — with all the hi-tech advantages of a computer. And because it was "old-hat" and mass-marketed, it was affordable by even the lowliest writer or mini-business office.

The PCW8512 comes with a dot-matrix printer; the newer PCW9512 with a daisywheel printer. both use the CP/M operating system and a word processor program called Locoscript (now version 2). Both use small, three-inch, well protected data-storage disks, used by Amstrad — and virtually no other manufacturer.

"The Amstrad" will do more than "mere" word processing however; various other programs are available — for data-base, a spread-sheet, accounting, etc. But these are all rather more difficult to use than the word processing for which the machine is specifically designed.

If your mini-business needs more than fairly standardised word-processing and the minimum of other applications, you should consider a more powerful personal computer.

Choosing a computer

There is a saying in the computer world that "No-one ever got the sack for buying an IBM." And the IBM personal computer, the original PC, (and its more recent, more advanced, replacements) is still the "industry standard". It has many close rivals though, and the standards are forever changing, the operations getting faster and more efficient. But – again thanks initially to Alan Sugar of Amstrad — it is possible to buy an "industry standard" type of computer for a much-lower-than-IBM price.

Many mini-businesses will find that their needs are fully met by an Amstrad PC 1512, the cheapest; or by an Amstrad PC 1640, a slightly more powerful and clearer-screened version. (I use a PC 1512 myself and am completely satisfied with it. It does everything that I need as a writer. Again, this is now far from "state-of-the-art", but who cares?) Some mini-business operators may decide that they need the newer Amstrad PC 2000 series which are much more up-to-date — but less competitive on price. Or, of course, there are other makes — which are now beginning to get quite close to Amstrad prices.

It is important to remember though that, unlike "the Amstrad" — the PCW 8256, 8512 or 9512 — the PC machines do not come complete. All you get is the computer, the keyboard (usually), the disk drive(s) and sometimes, but by no means always, the monitor. Merely to do word processing, you also need to buy a monitor (if necessary), a printer and — the absolute essential — a word processor program.

Let us therefore momentarily consider a few representative prices — which, inevitably in a highly volatile market, are only in round terms:

Amstrad PCW8512 — double disk drive, dot matrix printer, complete and ready to switch on
... around £400 + VAT

Amstrad PCW9512 — double-disk drive, daisy-wheel printer, complete and ready to switch on
... around £400 + VAT

Amstrad PC1512 — with double 5.25″ disk drive, keyboard, monochrome monitor and a "thrown-in" word-processing program
... around £480 + VAT

Plus ...
Amstrad dot-matrix printer .... around £200 + VAT
Reasonable package therefore .... around £680 + VAT

Amstrad PC1640 — double disk drive, keyboard, monochrome monitor
... around £550 + VAT

Plus . . .
Printer, as above
Package therefore .... around £750 + VAT

Amstrad PC2086 — with double 3.5″ disk drive,
  keyboard and monochrome monitor
                               . . . around £680 + VAT
Plus . . .
Printer, WP program, etc .... around £320 + VAT
Package therefore .... around £1000 + VAT

(And, if you are going for the 2000 series you are likely to opt for a machine with a hard disk — which will cost around £300 more than the double disk drive version.)

Clearly, you need to think very carefully about your needs before you move up-market. And most makes are more expensive than the Amstrad.

Programs

There are many word processor programs available for the "industry standard" PC and some of the less expensive ones — suitable for a mini-business — are listed in *Figure 4.3*.

If you decide that your mini-business warrants more than "just" a word processor, and opt for one or other of the more powerful personal computers, you must think about these other uses. Some of the commoner, other-than-word-processing, uses of a PC are:

Database: A database program is an electronic card-index system; a major difference is that with a computer database system you decide how big the "cards" are to be — and you can change your mind as the system grows. You can design the "cards" yourself, to fit your needs exactly. And, particularly useful, once the data is recorded, you can ask for listings by specified conditions

— for instance, list all entries with surname Bloggs, living in Muddlecombe, aged over 73.

Figure 4.3 lists a few simple and inexpensive database programs for the ordinary PC.

Spreadsheet: A spreadsheet program is like a large sheet of paper divided into columns and rows —which can be used, for instance to list various items of income and expenditure month by month. The real advantage of a spreadsheet however is its ability to perform calculations on the contents of the table. You can estimate sales in January, tell the program to use this figure as a model for other months, and then be shown the overall year-end effect. All in seconds. It is a very useful tool for preparing your business plan —and for updating it.

A few simple, inexpensive, spreadsheet programs for the PC are also listed in *Figure 4.3*.

Accounting systems: programs are available that will take full care of everything to do with the payroll, keep tags on investments, or handle tax and VAT matters.

The accounting programs are too varied to list in Figure 4.3 — you will do better to ask around at computer software dealers.

Desk-top publishing: You don't need to go into the real publishing business to take advantage of these programs. The simpler ones are ideal for producing photocopiable "masters" of single-sheet advertising material, small (A4 size) posters, or simple three- or four-page news-letters.

I have one of the simplest such programs — NewsMaster II, which costs about £70 — and have used it to produce publicity material about my lectures. Unless your mini-business is about publishing, nothing more sophisticated is justified — but this simple program could be of value to any mini-business. And it is very simple: you will find that you can use it literally within minutes of opening the box.

Figure 4.3. A very personal selection of inexpensive programs for mini-business use with a "standard" PC. (Prices are for 1989 "order of cost" and exclude VAT.)

Word Processors

Tasword PC: excellent value, very fast, no spelling checker included, but available at extra cost...................................... *£30*

WordStar Express: a very good budget version of what was for years the "industry standard". Easy to use................................ *£60*

Topcopy Plus: very fast operating, can have three files on screen at same time, includes spelling checker. *£100*

Multi-writer 2: very powerful (which means it will do a lot more than just process words), includes a spelling checker — and a pop-up calculator too. *£115*

Sprint: extremely fast, integral thesaurus as well as a "while you type" spelling checker, automatic saving of work in progress. *£200*

Databases

dBaseIV — the "industry standard". *£350*

DBXL (Version 1.20) — great value for money, all the power of the earlier versions of dBase (eg, dBIII). *£90*

Tas Plus — a friendly, less powerful, version of the £500 **Tas Professional**. Ideal for mini-businesses. *£120*

Filer 1295 — very simple, "friendly", but limited (only 10 entries per "card"). But very cheap................................. *£12.95*

Figure 4.3 continued

Spreadsheets

Lotus 1-2-3 (Version 2.01) — the "industry standard" — 8192 rows and 256 columns. £250
The Twin (just what it says — a twin of Lotus 1-2-3) — but look at the cost.................£70
Twin Special Edition — much the same, but "only" 1000 rows and 256 columns, and cheaper still. £35
Planner 1295 — basic, but easy to use, and cheap...............................£12.95

Integrated Packages

Never forget the excellent programs contained within various inexpensive integrated packages.

Mini Office Personal: word processor plus database, spreadsheet, communications package, label printer and "utilities" program — *all* for £30
Eight-in-One: word processor with spelling checker plus spreadsheet, database, graphics, an outliner programmer, a communications program and a desktop utilities program (Calendar, memopad, clock, etc.). And all for £40
And my own, now somewhat long-in-the-tooth, favourite:
PC-Four: includes the excellent *Quill* word processor — well, its the only one I really like for my own use, no spelling checker but so-o-o easy to use and ideal for a writer — plus excellent spreadsheet, database, and graphic design programs. Far more than I need —for £50

Figure 4.4 An example of what can be produced using a PC, a simple desk-top publishing program — in this instance, NewsMaster II — and a 24-pin printer.

Amaze your friends !
Become a published writer !
Learn about :

WRITING AND SELLING MAGAZINE ARTICLES

A Saturday course, by **Gordon Wells**

Genius is not necessary - just application. If you can write an interesting letter, you can write an article.

Who by? Gordon Wells, author of THE CRAFT OF WRITING ARTICLES and THE MAGAZINE WRITER'S HANDBOOK, is giving a conentrated one-day course of four lectures - for beginners and others . . .

Where, When and How?

At Forest Community School, Horsham, Saturday, 32 March 1999.

10.00 am to 4.00 pm. Fee £10.00. Contact: Horsham 9978203

Figure 4.4 is an example of what can be done with NewsMaster II — using an ordinary PC 1512 and a 24-pin dot-matrix printer.

Communications: It is possible to link your computer with others, via the telephone system. To do this, you need a *modem* — a device which translates electronic signals so that they can be transmitted down the telephone line — and a communications program. With this equipment, you then subscribe to an electronic mail (e-mail) system, and can transmit material direct from your computer to that of other subscribers. You can also gain access to vast libraries of computerised information.

But *e-mail* is a specialised subject; communications programs are therefore not listed in this book. Seek specialist advice.

Other office equipment

Personal computers are undoubtedly important — and increasingly so. But they are not the only items of sophisticated office equipment that a mini-business-person needs to think about.

Photocopiers and *fax* machines are becoming more and more within the financial reach of a one-person mini-business. But they are only warranted if the business is such that they are necessary. (I get on fine without either — my local library offers photocopying facilities at 5p a sheet.)

Everyone knows what a photocopier is. The important points to note about these machines are that they are now significantly cheaper, and to avoid other than plain-paper copiers. Cheap machines that copy on special thermal paper are usually a bad investment. The plain-paper copier is the standard. A good quality, A4 only, plain paper copier, suitable for most mini-businesses, can be purchased, at the time of writing, for around £500 + VAT.

Unlike photocopiers, *fax* is new to some people. Effectively, a fax machine "photocopies" an original document and transmits it, electronically, down the telephone network to another fax machine, anywhere in the world, where the original is reproduced in moments — as a photocopy. There is an international standard, so fax machines can all communicate with each other — although some are slower than others. All you need is a telephone line.

The older telex system entailed the physical typing of material into a special machine; the newer *e-mail* too entails the original being already on, or loaded via, the computer; fax however will transmit photocopies of drawings, signatures, antique book pages — anything. More and more businesses have fax terminals.

Some fax machines have a facility for automatic transmission of material at more economic off-peak times. Most can also be used as office photocopiers. But fax output is usually on thermal paper; plain paper machines are considerably more expensive. At the time of writing, one or two small, "personal", fax machines are available at around £600 + VAT.

Before buying (or leasing) either a photocopier or a fax machine, be sure to investigate more than just the initial capital cost. The copier will need replacement cartridges (containing the toner — the "ink") and the fax machine will need rolls of thermal paper. Check the operating costs before you plunge in.

Investigate too the possibility of buying a fax facility (on what is known as a "card" which is plugged in inside the computer) to link with your PC — it could save a lot of money.

An office system

And finally, for this chapter, let us come right down to earth and think about the mundane business of filing.

We have already mentioned the importance of a reliable filing system to any mini-business. But most people hate filing. So what is the minimum you can get away with?

I suggest that you start by buying a number of large lever-arch files (and a filing punch).

On the accounting side, you will need to retain the receipts for all the purchases you make; you will also need to keep copies of all invoices you issue. I suggest a file for each — and I put paper separators at the end of each calendar month. (I use thin — "Bank" — coloured A4 sheets turned on their side, so that they project out from the other papers in the file.)

The number of files you require for correspondence will depend on the nature of your mini-business. You may be able to manage perfectly well with a single file, with all incoming letters and copies of your own, outgoing, letters merely filed in date order. (I can still manage with little more than such a system — I have just two correspondence files. I deal, mostly with a few magazines and two or three publishers.)

This simple system is fine when you are dealing with only a small number of correspondents. But if your business is such that you correspond with a large number of suppliers and purchasers, you will need separate files for each correspondent. Then, thinner cardboard files are more appropriate.

You may also decide that you need to keep a single large file of copies of all your outgoing letters — as well as the copy filed by correspondent. This will often help you find a letter more quickly — if someone phones, and you cannot easily get to the filing cabinet, you can often just reach for your handy file of "daily" letters.

If your files are very numerous, you will need a filing cabinet — in which you should store them all, alphabetically. Don't invent a personalised, non-alphabetical system. It's bound to go wrong. Just keep it simple. *Figure 4.5* contains advice on organising a filing system.

Figure 4.5. Organising the filing system

Adopt an alphabetical basis for the filing system:

- File by name, alphabetically, and read as many letters as necessary to establish precedence — thus Smith is filed before Smitt.
- For individuals reverse the surname and first names — thus, Henry Smith is filed as Smith, Henry.
- For businesses, do not reverse names unless they are surname and first name — thus Smith & Jones Ltd is filed ahead of Smith, Henry John, Ltd (the & is read as "a-n-d").
- Read all names where necessary to establish order — thus Smith, Henrietta is filed before Smith, Henry (the second e in Henrietta takes precedence over the y in Henry).
- File initials only, before full names — thus Smith, H is filed ahead of Smith, Henrietta.
- File shorter forms before longer — thus Smith, Henry is filed before Smith, Henry J and Smith before Smithers.
- Treat compound and hyphenated names as single names.
- If dealing with more than one office of the same firm, file by the firm's name in full and then the letters of the branch name (location) — thus Henry Smith Plc (Brighton) is filed ahead of Henry Smith Plc (London).

Figure 4.5 continued.

Do not have any "Miscellaneous" files:

- These can be a graveyard for lost records.

Make EXTRA files:

- There is no law that says you can only have one copy — you can also make photocopies. File one copy of all correspondence under the name and, if likely to be ongoing and important, another under the topic.

- "Daily" files — all correspondence on each day, filed solely in date order. (Maybe also file photocopies of incoming correspondence — by receipt date — but this is less important.) Empty out "daily" files after a few months — they are only of value when instant access is needed, while a topic is "hot".

Clip (or stick) small but important papers to A4 sheets:

- Small pieces of paper can easily get lost in a big file. They may be just as valuable/important as bigger sheets. Safeguard them.

And files are of no use at all if not kept up-to-date — and reviewed regularly. Work on your filing system. It will pay off.

CASE STUDY – *Michael*

Michael lost his job as a senior chemist in the rubber industry about six years ago, in his early fifties; he was considered "too old" to get another job in the same field; so he set up his own business. Now, he runs a successful specialist mini-business, processing and printing black-and-white films. He operates as a "sole trader" but, sensibly, employs his wife at just below the wage level at which National Insurance contributions are required.

When he started his mini-business, Michael had not processed films or prints other than for himself. But he had a lot of experience as an "amateur" — he knew how to do it. Before he started, he prepared a business plan which he discussed with a counsellor from the Small Firms Advisory Service. Armed with his detailed plans, Michael then obtained the Enterprise Allowance: within three months he was no longer reliant on this.

Today, the business is the main means of support for Michael and his wife. Turnover is held to just below the VAT registration level (currently £23,600). Were he to be VAT registered, this would mean increasing his prices — and he would have all the extra work of keeping VAT records; he was strongly advised by his accountant to avoid VAT registration. Overall, the business achieves a net profit (after all costs, which include paying his wife) of about 30 per cent of turnover — on which they live. And he is now buying a tax-efficient self-employed pension.

Business comes from personal recommendation and from regular small advertisements in the photographic press. Michael has a neatly printed and very detailed price list which he updates annually (out-of-date prices mean business losses); this is sent to all customers and — for a stamped addressed envelope — to enquirers.

Michael works from a building in the garden which serves as darkroom, print finishing room and office. For this he had to seek planning permission before starting work. His mini-business required more than two thousand pounds worth of equipment, beyond what he already had, but he was able to manage without a loan. he also had to pay for the building from which he operates. His own capital was supplemented by an £800 grant from the Local Authority.

From the start Michael recognised that to make a go of his mini-business, he had to work long and hard. When he started, he worked twelve hours a day, 8.00 am to 8.00 pm, seven days a week; recently though he has slowed down — he works the same hours but now takes Sundays off. And if his wife were not working with him, he just couldn't cope with the work. There aren't enough hours in the day.

Michael is content with his mini-business, and if he had his time over again, he would do the same thing — but would start younger. His advice to those about to start their own mini-business is:

- start by researching the market very carefully, and preparing a realistic, business plan;
- self-discipline and motivation are essentials — you must be prepared to work very long hours;
- the business must always come first — don't let yourself be distracted by the home surroundings;
- keep finances tight and under strict control — never spend more than you earn;
- always take all the help you can get, and never be too proud to seek advice;
- accepting all that, if you will persevere and can retain your confidence . . . then you *will* succeed.

5
THE END PRODUCT OR SERVICE

Let's go back, for a moment, to basics. You are engaged in your mini-business for fun and profit. The fun comes easy — when you're not tearing your hair out with worry and/or frustration. The profit you have to work at. And to make a profit, you have got to sell your product or service.

Whatever your product or service, you have got to get out there and sell it. And because we have defined a mini-business as usually a one-person outfit, that *you* really means YOU. There is seldom scope for you to take someone on, to do the selling for you.

(Your business will almost certainly be too small, for many years, to be able to afford a salesperson anyway. Any salesperson is going to look for an income — from salary and commission — of at least £10,000; and there will be expenses on top of that — car, insurance, etc. So forget about a salesperson. And even an agent — as in eg a writer's agent — is going to take a percentage. Until you have proved your ability, you can't afford an agent. Not only that: you'd have a job finding one to take you on.)

Selling

So . . . no matter how "creative", "artistic", or just plain shy you may be, you have to get personally involved in the business of selling.

First, how are you going to sell your product or service? Are you going to sell your professional services largely to business firms — as in management consultants or lecturers, computer programmers and PR people? Are you going to sell a skilled, finished product to one or two big organisations — as in writers selling to a publisher and a couple of magazine editors? Are you going to sell your creative work direct to the public, but through a retail outlet — as in artists selling through a gallery?

Or are you going to manufacture something — pots of "home-made" jam, individual house-name-plates, or sandwiches? And do you propose to sell these products direct to the public or sell them, on a wholesale basis, to retail outlets?

If you propose to sell direct, how? Will you sell from a market stall or car boot, or from your working premises, or will you sell by mail order? This latter option gets you into the advertising business — and we shall look into that a little more in the next chapter.

The answers to all the above questions will affect how you proceed. You *should* have thought all of them through already, while you were working up your business plan. Even if you did, give them further thought now.

If you are selling a service, what is the buyer looking for? In a nutshell:

- a service which can't be done — at all, or as cheaply, or as efficiently — in-house;
- quality work — better advice, writing, artwork, etc.;
- delivery on time.

If you are selling one-off products such as commissioned books or magazine features, you are in a very similar situation to the mini-business-person above, who was selling a service. The publisher/editor basically looks for (but doesn't always get in entirety):

- a unique piece of creative work
- marketable quality
- delivery on time

Notice the similarity in requirements — quality work, on time. Money is usually of secondary importance —to the buyer, not to you.

If you are going to sell your manufactured product on a wholesale basis, to retail outlets, the buyer's requirements will be somewhat different. The shop's buyer will want:

- a product that looks good — and that *sells itself* (When did a salesperson last sell you something you weren't already looking for — or at least, thinking about?);
- an exclusive product — at least within that town;
- something small and compact that is good value for money in terms of occupied shelf space;
- a product that will not go out of fashion (remember hula hoops?), or deteriorate on the shelf;
- a product that can quickly be replenished — if the shop sells out, it will want quick delivery of more stock;
- a profitable product (an acceptable margin).

Notice that now, price is more important; so too is appearance — which should symbolise quality — and again, delivery on time.

And finally, in this appraisal of the mind of the buyer, let us consider direct sales from stall, car boot, atelier, or your own mini-business mail order process. Now the shopper's requirements are:

- a good quality product — that will wear well and, depending on what it is, not go out of fashion, at least not too quickly;
- a bargain — which might mean no more than "something that can't be obtained elsewhere", which brings us on to "exclusivity";
- immediate delivery.

Again — quality and time are paramount.

Marketing policy

Having briefly reviewed the requirements of the different buyers, let us think about how you are going to meet them, and how you are going to compete.

If you are "manufacturing" a small product — a pottery mug is a good example — you cannot hope to compete with the price of a factory-produced mug. Why not? Because the factory produces mugs in large numbers — all identical. To compete, you must offer either something better or something more exclusive. And if your mugs are better and/or exclusive, you will be able to charge more for them. So long as they are good value for money and will sell well, the shopkeeper is likely to be interested only in maintaining the *profit margin* per item.

You need to think too about your own price. If the factory-produced mugs are sold to the shopkeeper at 40p each for sale at 60p (plus VAT), this is a *mark-up* of 50% on cost, or a *profit margin* of 33.33% on selling price, before VAT. Add VAT (at 15% say) to that and the price to the customer is 69p. That is the figure you will see on the price-tag.

Suppose you judge that your mugs will sell — on quality and exclusivity grounds — for £1.20. (You've seen other hand-made mugs, not as good as yours, selling for about that price.) You must offer the shopkeeper the same percentage mark-up. So you need to work back from your chosen "shelf-price" of £1.20 to get the price you can charge the shopkeeper.

First, take off the VAT: divide the £1.20 by 1.15 (or 1.10 if VAT is 10%, etc.) to get the pre-VAT price of £1.04. Now divide that £1.04 figure by 1.50 (the .50 being the 50% mark-up mentioned above) to get the price you can charge the shopkeeper — which works out at just over 69p. Round it off to 70p. Check your calculations: 70p plus 50% mark-up on cost equals

£1.05; add 15% VAT to that to get a price-tag of just under £1.21. (The shopkeeper will undoubtedly call it £1.20 and accept a mark-up of a tiny fraction under 50%.)

Now think carefully. Can you produce your mugs — *and maintain your own profit margin* — to sell at 70p? If not, maybe you will have to sell them direct. Or maybe you should try to negotiate a lower margin with the shopkeeper — surely a proposition unlikely to succeed. (He is more likely to be looking for a better margin — on the grounds that your mugs are tying up more of his capital per area of shelf space.) Or maybe the shopkeeper will be able to sell them at a higher shelf-price.

If you are selling a service — management consultancy, PR services, computer programming expertise, lecturing or writing — the price calculations are different. Basically you need to judge just how high a price to charge; the "purchaser" of your services will not be selling them on. You merely have to satisfy the purchaser that you are providing good value for money. The greatest danger of all is that you may sell yourself short, and charge too little for your expertise.

If you are selling a feature article to a magazine or a book to the publisher, you have little to think about — and little room to negotiate. Magazines tend to pay on their own take-it-or-leave-it judgement of the worth of your work; publishers usually pay somewhere around "industry standard" royalties on sales. (Although of course, advances — payments "up front", against royalties to come — vary widely.)

Back with the mugs, the shopkeeper will not just want to sell one or two of your product. If your mugs are of better quality and perhaps more ornately sculpted than the factory product they will sell quite well. But the shopkeeper will want assurance that you can maintain a supply. Deliveries of six mugs this week, none the next, two the following week and then perhaps two dozen the week after will not match up with the shop's sales pattern.

If your mug-making mini-business is to succeed, you must commit yourself to producing a reasonably fixed number of mugs per week. (A variation in production between say 6 and 10 may be acceptable; a variation from zero to 24 is not.) The number need not necessarily be great, but the shopkeeper will want an assurance of supply.

Indeed, a steady supply of three hand-made quality products per week may, of itself, justify a higher price for "exclusivity".

In the last few paragraphs, we have also really been talking about delivery times. The shopkeeper needs to know that around mid-morning each Tuesday say, a fresh supply of your "Marvellous Mugs" will arrive. If deliveries are sometimes Tuesday, sometimes Wednesday, and very occasionally Monday or Thursday, the shopkeeper cannot plan his sales: he cannot tell a "sold" customer to come in on Tuesday afternoon to collect. Disappointed, time-wasted, customers are easily lost.

If you are selling a service (eg computer programming) or service-oriented product (eg a book or magazine feature), delivery timing is equally important. Even if you have to work late into the night, or miss a favourite television programme, or even a planned holiday, you MUST complete your work on time.

Think of a magazine editor sending the magazine off to be printed; your feature article has not arrived, as promised, yet it has been "trailed" in the previous issue. The editor cannot hold up production for the delivery of your material. Something else has to be slotted in at the last moment — out of the "reserve" stock; and thousands of expectant readers (well, a couple of them anyway) will be disappointed. You'll have to be very lucky to get any more commissions from that editor.

Think of a firm about to launch a major new sales campaign; a small part of the campaign depends on the timely arrival of the program you have been commissioned to write. You haven't finished debugging it. Do they proceed with the (fractionally) incomplete package, or hold everything up for you to finish your work? Whatever the decision, next time they will look elsewhere for their programming needs.

Don't commit yourself — and your mini-business to delivery or completion dates you can't meet. But once committed, you MUST deliver.

One last thought about marketing policy: you need to *stay* in touch with market needs. You must have an ear to the ground all the time.

You will have done your basic market study when preparing your business plan. But the needs of the market are forever changing. You must forever be prepared to adjust your product to changing demand. (Again, remember hula-hoops. If your mini-business was engaged in making hula-hoops and you had not stayed in touch with the market, you might still be making them. Or already be bankrupt.)

Let us now consider the matter of presentation, or packaging. In a mini-business, you need to think about packaging the product, the mini-business as a whole, and yourself in particular. First, the product.

Packaging the product

We have already mentioned how important the appearance of your product is to the shopkeeper. But the overall quality of your product is also of considerable importance, irrespective of the sales outlet. And views on the quality will certainly be influenced for the better if your work is presented well — ie, "packaged".

Your mugs — and other similar products — will often

sell better if they are boxed. Putting a mug in a box sets it apart from other, "cheapo", products.

Unless you are an artist, do not design the box yourself. Don't leave it to the printer, or box-maker, either. Find yourself a graphic designer and commission an appropriate box. (Maybe a square box — printed with your own mini-business "corporate" *logo* — but with the handle accessible through a cut-out corner? Nice gimmick. And gimmicks are important.)

Another nice packaging idea that I have just read about for selling home-made jam, is to add a distinctive cloth bonnet to the jars. Again, just a gimmick, but it may help to catch the shopper's roving eye.

Packaging is equally important in service mini-businesses.

If you are in the business of lecturing, offer handouts — and ensure that they *look good*. Handouts are taken away; they are what the students remember you by.

If you offer management advice — of any sort — on a consultancy basis, make sure that your report looks good. Don't submit advice or recommendations merely in the form of a letter — unless it's been a very small job. Submit a formal report. A report gets noticed.

Your report will attract more favourable notice if it is well packaged. Don't just staple half a dozen pages of typescript together. Give the pages a cover. If you are doing a lot of such work, invest in a standard, glossy, printed cover — with space on it for individualising the report. Think about using plastic comb-type ring binding for the report. Or maybe thermal binding. Equipment for either process costs under £200.

If you are a photographer, consider delivering proof prints in a standardised bulk purchased, plastic album — with your name and address on it, of course. The proofs themselves will look better because of their packaging — and because it is easier to show them around, you may get more orders. Final prints should, of course, be nicely mounted. And how about throwing in a tiny reprint of the photograph — stuck on the outside of the envelope? (Again, nice gimmick. Gimmicks sell.)

If you are a writer there is little, if any, scope for personalising your presentation. Book and magazine typescripts must be submitted in a standard format.

What a writer can do though is to ensure that the final presentation is really neat. There should be no — or very, very few — corrections on the typewritten pages; the ribbon should be fresh and not faded; the paper should not be too thin and flimsy. And typescripts should never be bound — editors, publishers and printers need to deal with typescripts a page at a time.

Even a computer programmer can ensure that the programs are well documented (which could be an industry first), and packaged neatly.

Your business image

Particularly when you are offering a service, but also for products, you must ensure that your mini-business itself is well packaged.

Perhaps the first thing is to ensure that the mini-business has a good name. As we have already mentioned, as a sole trader, you do not have to use your own name — so long as it is made clear that you are "Bill Bloggs, trading as Marvellous Mugs".

Marvellous Mugs might indeed be a good trade name. But you must think carefully about the implications of the name you trade under. (The manufacturers of one well-known brand of contraceptives had to change its corporate name before the City would take seriously its proposals to diversify.)

The right name decided upon, the next step is to "put a shine" on the way you present that name. And, often, the first impression your mini-business will make on potential customers is by letter. Your letters must look good; they must always look businesslike and professional. Your business letters are your opening gambit, your primary showcase.

There are four ways in which the appearance of a letter can often be improved. Consider:

- the quality of the paper
- the design of the letterhead
- the layout of the letter on the page
- the content of the letter.

The paper you choose for your business letters must be of good quality. Too thin a paper gives the impression of meanness, a cheese-paring attitude to business; but too thick a paper may look over-ostentatious — and may push up your postage bills. Whatever you do though, don't select a paper of less than 70 gsm weight; that should be the minimum.

For business letters I use a 100 gsm "high white laid" paper by Conqueror — and a 70 gsm paper for invoices and the like. (To help you decide on the most suitable quality of paper to use, take note of the letters you receive from firms you are likely to deal with. Match their quality. It was right for them; it'll be right for you.)

Next, the printed letterhead. Yes, printed. If you have "an Amstrad" (the PCW 8512 etc.) — or even a more powerful computer with a simple desk-top publishing program like NewsMaster II — you may think you can make your own letterheading. Think again. You *can* "roll your own" of course — but the result just isn't good enough for your mini-business.

Depending on the activity of your mini-business your letterhead should be restrained or a bit "pushy". A management consultant, computer programmer or analyst, a lecturer, a writer, etc will do best with a very restrained, "professional" letterhead. (My own does not even announce that I am a writer; it merely gives my name and address. Note: not just my address.) If your mini-business makes cuddly toys, sandwiches or small pieces of furniture though, you can afford to — indeed, probably should — be more flamboyant in your letterhead. At least the "firm's" name writ large, and possibly even incorporating a business *logo* or illustration.

In all mini-business letterheads though it is safest to err on the conservative side; a brash, "over-pushy" image may take a lot of living down; an over-restrained one can easily be beefed up.

The layout of a business letter is most important. Business letters should seldom exceed a single sheet. And the typescript should be set out so that the page looks attractive. The basic principles of modern business letter layout are:

- "Block" the letter. That is, align the date, the recipient's address, the salutation, the heading, the content, and the final signature "block" all to the left margin. Do not indent anything — neither salutations, paragraphs, nor signature. (Some exclude the date and reference numbers from the "blocking" preferring to locate these near the right hand margin. I dislike this, but it is not uncommon.)
- Leave generous margins — left, right, top and bottom. Don't squeeze in the last few words by reducing right or bottom margins. Better, cut something out.
- "Balance" the letter within the page: try to achieve broadly the same amount of space above the letter itself as there is below it — ie, the space alongside the date, address and salutation, should roughly equal the space alongside and beneath the signature block. If the letter is particulary short, leave extra space at top and bottom, between address and salutation, etc. and at right margin, to centre the "text proper" as near as possible within the page. Few things look worse than

a short letter cramped into the top of a page which is then empty at the bottom.
- Leave a blank line between blocked paragraphs, between a salutation and heading, between heading and start of content, and between end of letter and signature block. When possible, allow more than one line of space around the salutation, etc. — but not between paragraphs, hold that to a single blank line.
- Omit line-end punctuation in addresses, salutation and signature block.
- Always include your name (and your company name if different) as part of the signature block.
- Match up the salutations and endings correctly: if you start with "Dear Sir", you must end with "Yours faithfully"; if you start with "Dear Murgatroyd", the ending has to be "Yours sincerely" (or the equivalent).
- It is increasingly the practice to address correspondents by their first name. In your first letter, you may like to enquire whether this approach is permissible/preferred.
- When addressing a lady of whose marital status you are unaware, it is *usually* safe to use the Ms form of address. But be careful: some will take exception to this ("new") form of address. One good way round the problem is to write to "Dear Joan Smith".
- Preferably type the date in the form 32 March 1999 and do not punctuate. Don't use the form March 32nd, nor — in my opinion — 32nd March. Do not abbreviate the date — type the month and the year in full. Never use numbers only (32.3.99 — and certainly not the American 3.32.99).

Figure 5.1 illustrates an atractive and acceptable layout for a business letter.

The actual content of a good business letter — how to plan it, how to string the words together effectively — is looked at in more detail in Chapter 7.

There are three other parts of your business image

Figure 5.1 An acceptable layout for a typical business letter.

31 March 1991   ← ***Date in full, no punctuation***

Henrietta Smith-Bloggs   ← ***Address — no punctuation***
   Senior Editor
Fullsome Book Company Ltd   ****Blank space roughly***
Globe Park Estate   ***balanced, top and bottom***
Marlow, Bucks XY8 2ZQ

Dear Hetty   ← ***All "ranged" to left margin***

THE MAXI-BUSINESS WORK-BOOK

Thank you for your letter of 15 March, reference HSB/73, and my apologies again for not phoning you earlier. My purpose now is merely to confirm what I said to you on the phone today.

Work on THE MAXI-BUSINESS WORK-BOOK is progressing well. I shall certainly be able to deliver the complete typescript by earlier than the contract deadline. I would not like — yet — to commit myself to delivering it a whole three months ahead of schedule. But I understand your reasons for asking for this speed-up and I shall do the best I can. I can already guarantee to deliver one month early, and I will now seek to revise some of my other commitments such that I can give you a further month's speed-up. I shall know the result of my commitment rescheduling within a week. I will write to you then, with a firm delivery date.

Let me say how much I appreciate your high opinion of my professionalism in even asking for this speed-up. With the two-month speed-up that I am hoping for, and your agreement to waive going to galleys, we should just make the deadline your American associates are setting. Give me a ring if you see any further problems.

Yours sincerely

                ↑ ***Text roughly centred on page***

                ****Blank space below***
Gordon Wells

that need consideration: the possibility of using a publicity brochure; the value of a business card; and . . . you yourself. The idea of a brochure, and other ways of getting publicity will be considered in detail in the next chapter. A business card is closely associated with yourself; it may be taken in to a client immediately before you are shown in; or you may proffer it yourself — as an *aide memoire*. Let us consider the need for a card in the context of the final section of this chapter — the section about you.

Your personal image

Not only does your mini-business have to give the appearance of professionalism, to look businesslike — so do you. You can be your own best — or worst — ambassador.

Imagine you are a potential client or customer. You are visited by the representative of a small firm seeking business. Your office door opens. In walks a scruffy-looking person in casual clothes and with untidy hair, carrying a tired plastic shopping bag. Are you likely to be favourably impressed and enthusiastic to talk business? Of course not.

If the representative is smartly dressed in more-or-less standard business clothes, is carrying a briefcase or the like, and looks neat, efficient and businesslike, you will at least listen with interest.

Maybe *manners maketh man,* but the right clothes certainly maketh a good impression too.

Not just clothes. When visiting a customer, your own person must be clean and tidy too. You may have taken your printing press or spinning-wheel to pieces over the weekend — but you must still have clean, unbroken finger-nails on Monday morning when you go a-calling. If you look scruffy or "down-market" you will be selling yourself short. And you may never live down that poor first impression.

Even your car, if it is going to be at all visible, will say something about you. It will not help your image as a business efficiency expert if you turn up at a client's office — and have to park your worn-out, dirty old (but not yet vintage) Beetle just under the MD's window.

And now, back to the visiting card. Get yourself a discreet one printed. No matter what your mini-business, let the accent be on the discreet. A business card need not — indeed, in my view, should not — incorporate a personal picture; but a very small company *logo,* yes. And do not give yourself a grandiose job-title. Your mini-business is a one-person affair: you need no title within it.

Finally, on the matter of your personal image, you must be prepared for anything. We will discuss how to best to get your sales point across to the customer in Chapter 8. For now though, it is important to be ready for whatever comes up when you meet a potential customer.

You need a briefcase — or larger, if your product demands it — stocked with everything you are likely to need. Adapt the following list of items to your own situation:

- your diary (or "personal organiser" = Filofax) in case you need to book a meeting or engagement, or agree and record a delivery deadline.
- if you offer a service — a printed sheet quoting the terms, conditions and fees you are prepared to work for. (And beware — don't undersell yourself.) If you vary your charges according to the client and the on-the-spot "feel" — as I do — at least have all the figures clear in your mind before you go — and confirm the agreed terms in writing immediately you get home.
- samples of your product:
  — anything from photographs of manufactured items

(or paintings), to actual sample goods;
  — anything from lecture handout sheets to published books;
  — anything from feature articles to press publicity cuttings;
  — anything from typical business reports to a portfolio of designs or photographs.
- a pocket calculator — to work out costs.
- your price lists and order forms — assuming you are seeking an order for your "manufactured" goods. And be sure that you know just what — unwritten — discounts you are willing to offer, to get a sale.
- visiting cards (see above) — valuable as an *aide memoire,* if nothing else.
- a note pad plus a *spare* pen and/or pencil. (A fold-over clipboard with a built-in pocket, is a useful way of ensuring that odds and ends are to hand.

Remember: you MUST be well organised. Everything must be to hand. If you do not project a good personal — and business — image, you may not get the work. The importance, to any mini-business, of the packaging of the product or service, and the "corporate" and personal image, cannot be overlooked.

Look good — sell well.

CASE STUDY *John*

John, now 40 years old, is a highly successful graphic designer. He started up in full-time business for himself eight years ago, having "tested the water" by home-working in his spare time for a couple of years before that. The business was a bit of a struggle for the first year, but during that time he had the financial support of his wife — who was then still a wage-slave.

Operating from a room at home and also from a rented office, John is a "sole trader". Working this way, he has less paperwork and less bureaucracy; and these are some of the things John left "wage-slavery" to escape. ("Office politics" was another.) And of course, he enjoys the independence of self-employment.

Being the boss of his mini-business gives John "the freedom" to work at least ten hours a day. Despite the long days though, he works a strictly five-day week — weekend working is out. (Well, nearly always.)

John has an efficient, well-set-up office, complete with all the usual electronic facilities: answering machine, "Amstrad", photocopier and fax machine; for his design work, he also has a specialist camera. Several of these items of equipment were included in a specially arranged office-leasing deal. But he didn't start out as well equipped as this: initially, he had only the minimum necessary equipment. In this way, he didn't need to borrow capital to start up the business.

In his area of work, John attracts business almost entirely through personal recommendations: he is "known". He does not need to advertise or circulate potential customers with brochures or whatever.

His mini-business is successful: John currently earns well over £15,000 a year. Inevitably, with this size of business, he is VAT registered. Very sensibly too, he is buying himself a self-employed pension. With no hesitation, if he had his time over again, John would start up his own mini-business — just as now.

John has good advice for those contemplating following in his footsteps:

- get a good accountant;
- don't let the paperwork "slip", or build up;
- invoice as soon as possible — and "chase up" payments, in a friendly manner;
  (John makes the helpful suggestion that with large organisations, it pays to build up a friendly relationship with someone in their accounts department.)
- don't overdo the hours — it's easy to "burn yourself out" — you *need* time off, to relax, to get "work" out of your head;
- if you get more work than you can handle, remember that there are always other freelance workers who will help, or to whom you can "farm out" some of the work.

6
MARKETING THE PRODUCT – ADVERTISING

By now, your mini-business is well and truly planned; maybe even under way. And you're going to make a fine product, offer a good service, are you not? That way, you'll make a good profit. Well no, not necessarily.

You'll never make a profit, never succeed at all in your mini-business if no one knows you're doing it. No one ever beat a path to an un-marked door. You have got to let your market know that you can offer what they want, what they need. Even perhaps, convince them that what they want is what you are offering. You have got, in the broadest sense of the word, to advertise.

Stewart H Britt, an American advertising consultant, put it rather well, back in the late 1950s. He said, "Doing business without advertising is like winking at a girl in the dark. You know what you're doing, but no one else does."

But advertising does not, for the mini-business, usually mean full-page display ads in the newspapers or expensive mini-stories in the TV breaks. All it need mean is that you let your market know that you are able to supply their needs. The advertising needs of a mini-business may well be minimal; they can never be non-existent. Someone has to know you are in business; if not, how do you get any work or sales at all?

Even the artist, delivering a painting to a gallery has had — in a very small way — to advertise.

How does the artist know that the gallery will accept his/her pictures for display? Probably there was a prior visit or phone call. In the broadest sense of the word, that's advertising — the artist has to go to, or call up, the gallery and say, "Hallo. I'm an artist. Will you display, or buy, or market my work?"

Without that approach, the gallery might not have known of the artist's existence. And merely by displaying the artist's work in the gallery, where people know they can come and see new work, they in turn are advertising it.

Mini-business advertising then, in the broadest sense of the word, can come in a variety of forms:

- simple letters or phone calls to already-known contacts in the relevant business;
- sales letters to likely clients/customers in the relevant business;
- a printed brochure, mailed to likely clients/customers;
- advertisements in specialist publications;
- press releases and PR-inspired "news".

Let's look at each of those advertising opportunities in more detail.

Contacts

Certainly for a service mini-business, who you know is of immense importance. You are more likely to get business from people who already know you — at work.

It is not unusual for a large business to encourage its staff to set themselves up as mini-businesses to which the parent firm then contracts out their past duties. This is the ideal use of prior contacts.

(One large firm with a household name in the photocopying equipment business has over fifty former employees now operating as a network of mini-businesses contracted for part of their time to the parent firm. Changing from direct employment to contracted mini-businesses generated a significant saving in the parent's overheads. Most of the hived-off mini-businesses have prospered — some spectacularly — and none have failed. Their activities range widely from staff training through PR work to computing. The parent firm deliberately contracts for no more than 50 per cent of the time or output of any one mini-business. That way, the offshoots have to become truly independent. These successful mini-businesses show the benefits of maintained contacts.)

When I retired from full-time wage-slavery, to write and lecture on my own behalf, one of my first actions was to make contact with a few old friends — who could conceivably use my lecturing services. Some took up my offer — one-day courses in letter and report writing and in making an oral presentation — and I was launched. (And of course, I also had a commissioned book to get on with. And ideas for more.)

Had I not overcome my innate reserve and written to my friends, I would not yet be earning money as a lecturer. And I have got other work — as a spin-off from those original lectures.

The moment you make the decision to establish your mini-business, start keeping notes of contacts: people who might be interested in your product/service; people to advise that the business you spoke about has now been launched. Build up a list of contacts. And use them.

No matter what your business, some of your friends will be interested. Ignore those butterflies in your stomach — contact your friends, tell them what you are doing. They may have been searching for a long while for an enamelled brooch, a stuffed toy — or someone to write that program for them. You'll never know, unless you tell them what you're doing.

The sort of letter you write to your friend-contacts will

to some extent depend on the degree of friendship. Certainly, the "top and tail" of the letter should be very personalised. The basic content however needs to spell out very clearly what you are doing. It will be much like the straight sales letter you write to other potential clients/customers. Let us therefore look at how you contact those you do not know — and then come back to the letter to friends.

Sales letters

The personalised computer-produced sales letter has become a bit of a joke since the *Reader's Digest* etc. began bombarding us all. ("Dear Mr Wells, You have been specially selected as one of the few people living in ABC Road, Muddlecombe, who will appreciate the . . ." And then you find that all your neighbours received similar letters.) But we are wrong to laugh at them. The *Reader's Digest* didn't achieve its huge world-wide sales by being ineffective. Those letters work.

So let us investigate how we might use at least some of the techniques of the conventional sales letter to publicise our mini-business. The only real change we need make is perhaps to be slightly less strident. The basic principles behind the pushy sales letter are equally valid for a mini-business though.

These basic principles are that:

- readers are basically interested in . . . themselves, and their own business. So you need to explain why they should be interested in what you are offering — ie, what's in it for them.
- readers are busy, and have a short attention-span — particularly when it comes to something they are not initially very interested in. So you need to interest them, quickly.
- readers are more likely to do as you wish if they are

told, very clearly, what to do. ("Return the enclosed form, now.")
- readers may not understand long detailed explanations. They certainly don't want to go into technical details. Your case must therefore be made as briefly and simply as possible.

The principles outlined above lead us to a recommended framework for a sales letter — a structure which can be remembered by the mnemonic HIBA:

H — the hook. The very first item in a sales letter should grab the reader's attention. If you delay it beyond the first few lines, the reader could well have thrown the letter into the wastepaper basket —without ever getting to the point.

I — the information. Now give the reader the facts; tell the reader what you are offering — your service or product. You might also, here, need to convince the reader of his/her need for what you are offering. (As in, perhaps, "Everyone needs a friend. Let me be your friend.")

B — the benefits. Knowing what you are offering is not enough; the reader wants to be told how your product or service can benefit him or her — personally (or in his/her business). The answer to "What's in it for me?"

A — the action. Fine, the reader is "sold"; now tell him or her what to do, how to go about achieving these benefits you have so clearly outlined. And the "when" should always be NOW.

To be effective, a letter needs a framework, a structure. Use the HIBA framework for your sales letters.

The "fancy blacksmith" of Chapter 2 might find it helpful to write a sales letter along the following lines:

Dear Householder

Does your house look just like all the others in the street? Wouldn't you like to make it look just a bit more personal? A <u>unique</u> — yes, <u>UNIQUE</u> — wrought iron name-plate would give your home that extra something.

I am a specialist: a Twentieth Century blacksmith. I don't rely on hot coals and hand-bellows; nor do I work under a spreading chestnut tree. I have a highly efficient — electronic — forge in my own modern smithy. And I work only to order. I don't mass-produce; nor do I have big business clients with a prior claim on my time. While I am working for you, <u>you are my only customer.</u>

Wrought iron name-plates, and support brackets for these and for porch lights, are the only things I make. I certainly don't shoe horses between jobs. By specialising in this way, I can guarantee the best — and at very competitive prices.

I will specially design, and make for you, a distinctive name-plate for your house, in good quality black wrought iron. Just tell me the house-name and I will send you a sketch design for your approval before I start working on it. There will not be another house name-plate like it — anywhere. I <u>guarantee this.</u> Your house name-plate will be UNIQUE to you.

Complete the enclosed form — tell me the name you want on the name-plate — and send it off ... NOW. You are not committing yourself to anything. Send no money, just the form.

Within a week I promise to send you a sketch design for YOUR name-plate and tell you how much it will cost. I know you will like the design — and the price. Until you agree with me though, you are committed to nothing — except having a look. You won't regret it.

Truly!

Lucius Longerfellow

On behalf of the blacksmith, I have attempted to "hook" the reader's attention in the opening paragraph. The desire to be different — yet similar — is a very strong emotion.

Notice too, how I have avoided using the cold and impersonal Dear Sir or Dear Madam (or even worse, the awful Dear Sir/Madam) in the salutation. Ideally, a sales letter should be addressed by name, but this is often impossible. Next best thing is to identify the addressee as directly as possible: Dear Householder, Dear Collector, Dear Managing Director or Dear Book Lover.

In the next paragraphs, I have explained how the new smithy is set up — given information about the mini-business. I go on, without a break, to stress the exclusivity and the really personal service — the benefit.

And finally, I press the hopefully now-interested reader to do something about it — but at the same time, offer the reassurance of "no commitment". With the design and the quotation there would be a really "hard sell" follow-up. You can't afford to lose the potential customer at that stage.

(An alternative approach worth considering, would have been to ask for a very small fee for the design, recoverable against the cost of the actual name-plate. The design fee makes the customer that bit more committed.)

In a sales letter like this you can break some of the rules of good business letter writing.

Underlining is now fully acceptable. (Ordinarily, underlining is the hall-mark of an amateur writer, who can achieve emphasis in no other way.) So too are capital letters — even the occasional exclamation mark. And you have to "beat the drum" a bit to get your point across.

Another definite "no-no" in ordinary business letters, which is permissible — indeed, highly recommended — in a sales letter is the hand-written PS. The space at the foot of the letter, near the signature, is important in its potential impact. Readers notice PSs — and particularly, written ones. So, in a sales letter (only) — always consider adding a personal PS.

(You might also consider a hand-written note at the other impact spot (at the top, near the salutation), saying something like "Last chance for delivery before Christmas!" In sales letters — for products, if not for professional services — you can usually afford to be really brash and pushy.)

Not used in this example letter, but of great value in sales letters generally, is the list. A list of benefits, services, past successes, etc. will have much impact. And the impact will be increased if the items in the list are highlighted with "blobs" (sometimes called "bullets") — as often used in this book. In a typewritten letter, use a lower-case O and carefully ink in the middle before despatch.

A sales letter advising potential clients of a more professional service would probably be better if a little more restrained — but nevertheless, it should follow the same framework. Whether trade or professional, the object is the same — to sell.

Now we can revert to the sales letter addressed to friends. For friends, the "fancy blacksmith" would need a different opening paragraph and a less "pushy" tail. But the material in the middle could be adopted as it is.

Follow-up by phone

Individual sales letters are all very well. Some will certainly succeed in seizing the interest of the reader to the extent that your offer is taken up. But many readers will get no further than just thinking, "Yes, that sounds good. I'll do something about that. But not now. I'm busy." A good mini-business-person goes beyond the mere sales letter. A follow-up by phone is often necessary — particularly with personalised letters.

There is a knack to following up sales letters by phone. There is a right and a wrong time too.

First, the timing. It would be pointless to phone before you send the letter. It is equally pointless — but slightly less obvious — to phone before the recipient can possibly have read it.

Think about when you posted the letters; make a realistic assessment of delivery time (by first or second class post?); allow for internal office delays (the mailroom, the busy secretary, etc.); and then for the recipient to find time to read it. To you, your letter is very important; to the business-person receiving it, it is just one more "sales-puff". It comes very low on the work priority list. Don't phone too soon.

At the same time, you do not want to delay your phone follow-up unnecessarily. If you leave it too long, the reader will have forgotten what the letter was all about. That would surely be a waste. The object is to call soon after the letter has been read; to reinforce the information or offer within it; to tip the balance in your favour. (Even, to persuade the recipient to fish it out of the waste paper basket.)

Before making your follow-up phone call, decide what you are going to say. Have a copy of your letter on the desk in front of you. Have all the facts at your fingertips — the person you are calling will undoubtedly seek clarification or further information about something. Have your diary ready too — and open. Be prepared to fix a deal on the spot — if you're lucky. Alternatively, and more likely, try to fix a meeting so that you can make a further, face-to-face "sales pitch".

Whatever you do, you must be persuasive. Don't be put off by initial lack of interest. Try to think of the one point that will seize your listener's interest. Remember the "What's in it for me?" principle.

Try not to let the phone call end without achieving something positive. If you don't get an actual order, say that you'll call back. If you get a firm rejection, and you are still convinced that this is a possible market, put the best face on it and say that you will come back to them in a few months' time — their needs may change.

Anything that you do agree over the phone should be confirmed — by you, in writing — immediately you put the phone down. Get in quick, before the client can forget.

Brochures

A sales letter may not be enough, on its own. Even with a telephone follow-up. Often, it will be worth sending out a printed brochure with the letter. Think of the sales letter as your salesman and the brochure as the salesman's samples or order book. Brochures are also particularly useful if your mini-business is offering a service rather than a product. Use a brochure where you want the recipient to retain a record of your available services.

An A4 sheet, printed both sides and folded in three makes an ideal brochure for the average mini-business. (It is important, in planning any postal sales campaign, to think about the total weight of the mailed material. Too elaborate a brochure — apart from probably not being the best value for money — may push the postage charges up into the next price bracket.)

Think carefully about the design of an A4 brochure. The first thing the reader will see is the front. That must make a bold and very brief statement — possibly, when offering a personal service, just your name, what you do, and a picture of yourself. The reader may also look at the back, before opening the fold. On the back you might put all the necessary factual information — your qualifications, address, phone and fax numbers, etc. Perhaps a potted biography too if relevant.

The next thing the average reader will do is to open the three-fold leaflet and look at the whole of the inside.

This inside spread is the place to do the "hard sell": to tell the readers what you are offering and how they would — certainly — benefit from it. Maybe you then want to lead them on to filling in an order form on the final third of the sheet; you must therefore complete your sales "pitch" in the top or left-hand two-thirds. (You must also ensure that nothing important, that you may want the reader to retain for reference, is on the reverse of the form. It is an ideal spot to mention any special extras — a bonus offer, a gift, etc.)

So . . . the layout of a two-fold, three-part brochure on a standard A4 sheet is to some extent determined. *Figure 6.1* illustrates a typical layout.

It is also important that you don't try to say too much in your brochure. The use of blank space and illustrations is as important as — if not more so than —the actual text. A good rule of thumb for brochure layout is to allow for 25 per cent of the available space to be left blank.

What you say on such a brochure will of course depend entirely on the activity your mini-business is engaged in. A freelance lecturer might usefully list his/her publications, list where he/she has already lectured, and list the topics about which lectures are offered. Fees are best not specified in the brochure.

For such a mini-business, the brochure is best printed in sufficient numbers to continue in use for some years (lecturers will not have a huge mailing list) thereby economising in printing costs; lecture fees however, will probably increase with inflation — and with a hoped-for demand for the lecturer's services. A separate typed and photocopied list of fees is therefore a sensible way of dealing with this. (Ideally, type the fees/price list on one-third of an A4 sheet — so that it fits neatly inside the folded brochure.)

For a mini-business with a large mailing list though, the brochure should be printed for just the one use — and include prices.

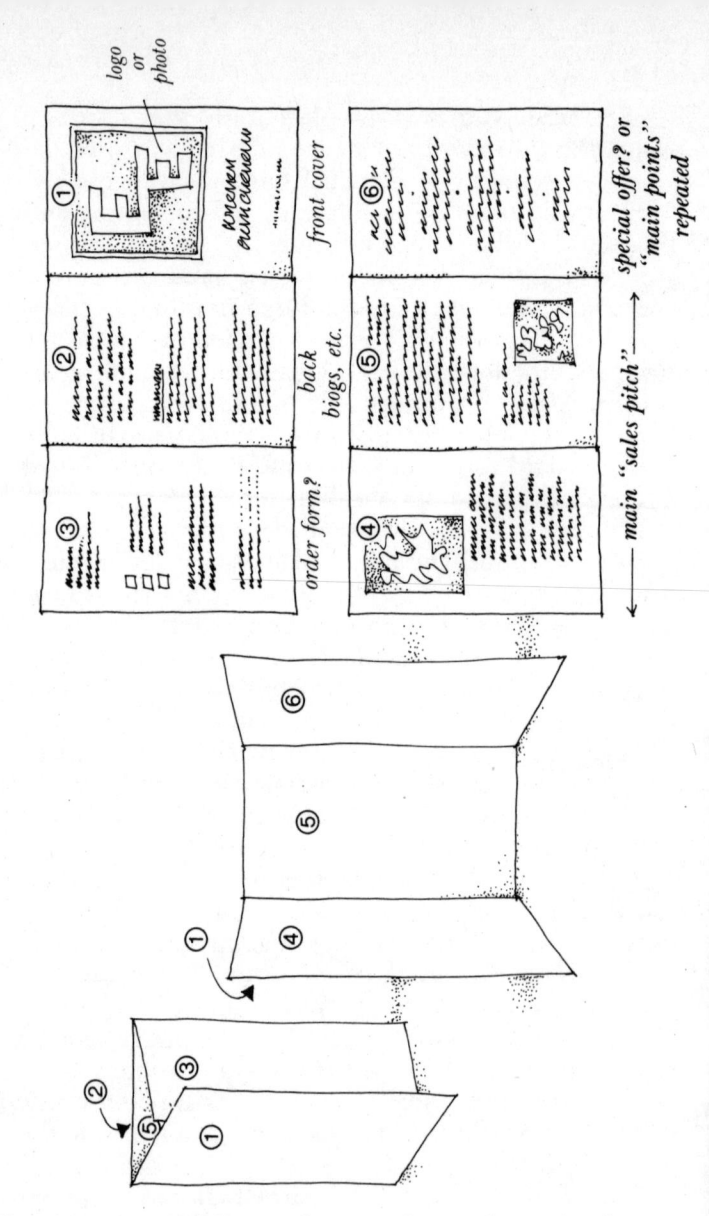

Figure 6.1 A typical layout of an A4 sheet to form a brochure — of a convenient size for posting.

Figure 6.2. Material for a brochure for a computer programmer, operating as a mini-business.

Page 1:

Logo (perhaps based on EE — for Egbert Efficiency) and/or photograph of self

For all your computer programming needs ...

Egbert Efficiency
33 Any Street
Anytown Anyshire AN93 0ZZ

Pages 4/5:

Egbert Efficiency is skilled in all the modern computer languages most used in business and technical environments. These include particularly:

- Fortran
- Rhubarb
- GM-Basic
- Cobol
- Pascal
- PML

Egbert Efficiency has worked for central and local government, and for many major business organisations, including:

- ABC Ltd
- OPQ and Partners
- XYZ (US) Inc

Original references from each of the above organisations can be seen at our offices.

Egbert Efficiency has personally developed one-off program suites for:

- Records and invoicing for an advertising agency
- Progress-chasing for a publishing company
- A major data-base of all business premises in a large district, for the relevant local government authority.

Just call in Egbert Efficiency and all your computing problems will be solved — effectively and speedily.

> The name is ... **EFFICIENCY!**

(Possibly, also include pictures of self, or a computer).

Figure 6.2 suggests what a brochure, for the computer programmer who we introduced in Chapter 2, might say on the most important pages.

Mechanics of mailing

We have talked glibly — above — of sending out a sales letter and a brochure. But it is not quite as straightforward as that. There are still three other matters to consider.

- who to send it to — ie, the scope of the mailing list?
- encouraging a reply — with a reply-paid envelope?
- the mailing arrangements — and the cost.

First, the mailing list. You may know who to send some of your sales letters to; but it is unlikely that you have a complete mailing list immediately to hand.

Over time, as your mini-business progresses — and hopefully flourishes — you will build up your own list of past and potential customers/clients. This list development is essential for any mini-business. People you have already satisfied will often come back for more. Add their names and addresses to your list. Keep them on the list for three or four "unproductive" years — thereafter, review their retention.

Without doubt, your own "home-made" mailing list is the very best you can get. But when you start, your own list will be small. You need to extend it.

Review relevant profession, trade, craft or hobby magazines; note likely names and addresses — from both display and classified advertisements. Study your local Yellow Pages directory; you should pick up many likely names and addresses there. (Your local library may have Yellow Pages directories for areas other than your own.) And use your initial mailing list itself to seek further names — ask "responders" to suggest friends likely to be interested.

Or you can buy a specific mailing list.

There are many firms in the business of marketing selective direct mail lists. Consult *The Direct Mail Databook* (Gower Press) or *Benn's Direct Marketing Yearbook* — in your local reference library. Alternatively, there are firms of List Brokers, who will find you just the right list; you can get a list of brokers from The Secretary, British List Brokers Association, 30 Eastbourne Terrace, London W2 6LG (Tel: 071-724 0560).

Such specialist lists are not cheap though: reckon on at least £100 per thousand names and addresses. (Consider carefully, whether the expense is justified. Your decision will depend very much on the type of mini-business you are in).

Think too, before starting off on your direct mail sales campaign, about encouraging replies — by enclosing a free reply envelope. There are two alternatives: the Business Reply envelope — which has to be specially printed; or the Freepost system — for which you do not need to supply the envelopes. You would need to consult the Post Office in either case.

And the need to consult the Post Office brings us on to our third "logistical" consideration. The Post Office — understandably — actively seeks to encourage direct mail sales campaigns. They offer a lot of advice on how to mount such a campaign and, for first-time users also offer a significant discount.

Any mini-business-person about to launch a direct mail sales campaign should consult the local Postal Sales Representative (at the nearest Head Post Office) for details of Royal Mail Direct Marketing Services. Ask particularly for a copy of their free — and very useful booklet *The Guide to Effective Direct Mail* and for their Introductory Offer Pack.

If direct mail advertising is likely to be of major importance in your mini-business, consider getting the *Post Office Direct Mail Handbook* (Exley Publications Ltd,

Freepost, Watford WD1 4WD: £12.95 plus £1.55 p & p.) It's a comprehensive "How To" book by experts.

Even if you don't want to get involved with mailing on the scale envisaged by the Post Office services, don't overlook direct mail selling. Get the free booklet for its advice, and run your own mini-campaign using ordinary stamps on ordinary envelopes. (On that scale, it has certainly worked well for me). Direct mail advertising is ideal for the mini-business — even if only on a tiny scale.

But there are, of course, other forms of advertising.

Advertising

You can advertise your product or service in magazines or local newspapers. Advertisements are expensive though. You must therefore ensure that they are effective. And the simplest advertisement, well-targeted, is usually the most effective.

How can you best target your advertisement? Ask yourself:

1 Who is most likely to buy my product/service?
2 Which publication are they most likely to read?

Simple questions, but too often overlooked.

If your potential market is local but of a general nature, such as all householders for name-plates or all parents for photographs of their children, consider advertising in the local newspapers. (Advertising in the local "freebee" may be cheaper — and possibly even more effective — than in the paid-for papers.) But if your potential market is specifically local photographers say, (eg, for hand-processing of films) you will probably be better advised to just contact the camera club secretary.

If however, you are offering your film-processing service to photographers nation-wide, a national advertisement is called for. Select your national photography magazine (say, the *Amateur Photographer*) and prepare to advertise therein.

A just-starting mini-business could probably not sensibly afford even a small display advertisement in the *AP*. But this is no problem. A cheaper classified advertisement in such a specialist journal is ideal. (Indeed, notice how many film processors do use *AP* small ads.)

You must make up your own mind — in response to the two basic questions posed above — about where to advertise. Wherever, think first about a classified advert. Display advertising is usually best left to bigger businesses.

The first basic rule for mini-business advertising is to use the most specialised publication possible, relevant to the product or service.

The second rule is to *maintain* the advertisement: don't advertise lavishly for just three weeks — and then go dead. It is much better to run a regular small ad than a one-off splurge. (Unless you get overwhelmed with work from the splurge.)

The wording of any advertisement — display or classified — should be short and simple. (Remember that with the multi-relevance mnemonic — KISS: Keep It Short and Simple.)

To advertise a film-processing mini-business for instance, decide on what is likely to be the most popular service, and advertise that — concisely. Offer details of other services in response to queries.

A processing advertisement might therefore read:

SPECIAL! *XP-1 develop & en-print: 24-exp £2.99; 36-exp £3.99 post paid. Fast turnround, individual processing. Other services: send sae. Smudgyprint, 99 Middle Road, Muddlecombe, Muds MC1 1XT.*

There is not one word too many in that small ad —

and it makes a strong point of the low price. It would attract custom. If you were offering a more cerebral service a phone number would probably be more effective. There is a useful implication of "DO IT NOW" about a phone number.

But advertising need not be exclusively of the paid-for variety. You can get your mini-business known of by it being mentioned in the news or features columns of magazines and newspapers.

Using the press

Just about any mention in the press of your mini-business — or, if like me you work under your own name, of yourself — is good advertising. So long as the mention is not too critical, the standard view of the acting profession is relevant: "It doesn't matter what they say, as long as they get your name right." So, how can you get these mentions?

You can get a press mention:

- by doing, or achieving, something news-worthy, or
- by writing a published feature.

To get into the news is not as difficult as it sounds. you can almost make a — local — news story just out of the fact that Bill Bloggs is setting up a new mini-business. More so if he is of retirement age. That might be sold as "Local pensioner starts new career". (Well, they do have to fill up all that space between the advertisements with *something*.)

But even that simple story won't get into the press unless the press is made aware of it. And that's where you come in. You must tell them. You might even write it yourself. You issue a *press release*.

Writing a press release is not like writing a letter. There are certain requirements to be met. And perhaps the most important requirement is that the story must actually be news-worthy. You starting up in business is highly marginal — but if you got a big order from China for your decorative mugs, that would almost certainly be (local) news-worthy. Remember, of course, that many press releases are not used: the editor doesn't consider them worth the space. There is nothing you can do about that — except, to make yours as interesting as you can. Just be prepared for disappointment.

Other features of a good press release are:

- it should be as brief as possible. About 200-250 words is an ideal length for a small press release. (If it's really world-shattering you won't need to write it yourself — just ring the paper up and they'll be round in a flash.)
- it should be written so that it can easily be cut back —from the bottom. So, put the really important fact(s) — the real meat — in the first paragraph; then expand and explain in subsequent paragraphs. Keep your paragraph lengths to about 50 words maximum. Use short sentences too — average 15 words. (But there is more advice on overall writing style in the next chapter.)
- it must be typed, on A4 paper, double-spaced, with large (around 50 mm) margins on all four sides.
- it should mention names whenever possible and indicate the connection of the named person(s) to the local area. (eg "William Shakespeare, 40-year-old freelance writer of 43 High Street, Stratford, has won a major literary prize for his new play, 'Hamlet'.") And, of course, when writing about yourself, do not refer to yourself as "I" but as "William Shakespeare" or whatever; ie, write in the third person.
- it must be factual — and, of course, accurate. A press release is not the place for opinion or conjecture.
- it must be news — not history. In other words, it is

no use offering a press release telling about something that happened last week. If possible, report something that is about to happen — and put an embargo on it until it is fact. (eg, "Local firm, Marvellous Mugs of Pottery Road, Muddlecombe today sold their thousandth mug to the Chinese government." Annotate that release with "Embargo until mid-day 14 March 1999 when mugs will be collected by Chinese representative." The press are used to such embargoes and will abide by them.)
- it must include, outside the text proper, the name and phone number of someone who can be contacted for further information. (Give the first name of the contact as well as the surname; the media work on first-name terms. A "Mr" Smith contact would grate.)
- the sheet of paper should be headed "Press Release" and ideally be on your business note-paper.

To write a feature for the press is a different skill. And it is not easy. It is of course easier for a writer than for our "fancy blacksmith". But even those "at ease with words" get articles rejected. To get your name into the press by writing features, you need to learn the trade.

If you feel the need to publicise your mini-business by writing articles about associated subjects, get my book: *The Craft of Writing Articles* (Allison & Busby). It's short, simple and straightforward — and very inexpensive. False modesty aside, I can honestly say that I don't know of a better one published in Britain. (There are excellent American books but their content is of limited relevance to British publications.)

Whenever I have a new book coming out, I always try to write at least one article about a relevant subject. This helps publicise the new book, and increases the sales. You can generate publicity, in just the same way, for your mini-business products or services.

All publicity is good advertising. And it costs very

little, apart from your time. It's not enough, on its own though. A mix of personalised sales letters and press mentions is the best way of making your mini-business a success. Adverts too — but only where appropriate.

CASE STUDY – *David*

About ten years ago, it looked as though the casino group for whom David worked would be taken over. The possibly unwelcome consequences of that — coupled with the wish to increase his income — led to his decision to start up his own printing and stationery supply business.

Still young, David spent four years building up his mini-business on a spare time basis. Then, six years ago, he went full time; the business is now his living. The first year of full time working was something of a struggle — too few orders coming in too slowly — but today the business is thriving. And he is still only 35.

Operating as a sole trader, David needed a loan of a couple of thousand pounds when he started up — to purchase printing machinery. Armed with his business plan, he approached his local bank; he reports that they "were very helpful, and gave him his loan immediately". His printing press, etc. are now set up in a workshop in his garden; "office work" is done from a spare corner inside the house. Office equipment is kept to the minimum —telephone (of course), typewriter and photocopier only; no more is necessary.

Much of David's business comes from the recommendations of satisfied customers —and from repeat orders. Living in a village though, it is worth David's while to run a continual small — and inexpensive — advertisement in the parish magazine. He is catering largely to a local demand.

The orders springing from these various sources are enough to keep David busy for about sixty hours a week. (No one ever said it wasn't hard work, working for yourself.) But the turnover of his mini-business is now coming up to a very respectable £35,000 a year. He is, of course therefore, registered for VAT — there are a lot of materials involved in the business.

Certainly, David is happy in his mini-business and, given his time over again, would do the same. His advice to those thinking of starting up their own mini-business is that they should:

- start part time and gradually build up the business until you can *see* enough income to go full-time;
- build up slowly and steadily — don't buy more equipment with borrowed money than is absolutely necessary;
- think about second-hand equipment — there are often real bargains in "good-as-new" items;
- get a good accountant — an accountant will save money in the long run (and help with the tax and VAT).

7
EFFECTIVE LETTER WRITING

We have already looked briefly, in the previous chapter, at the importance of one form of business letter — the sales letter. But in any business — including even a mini-business — there are always many other letters to be written. And ALL your letters are important: they are — initially at least — your ambassadors. On your letters shall you be judged.

If your business letters *look* sloppy, your whole business will be thought sloppy. We have already referred to the need for good presentation. But you must also think about what you say and how you say it. A poorly structured letter, confusing in its content, will do you no good at all: even if it does look attractive. It will be assumed — probably correctly — that your business too is disorganised and confused.

The answer therefore, is to ensure that your letters are models of good-looking, well-structured clarity. Think back to the all-purpose mnemonic we mentioned earlier: KISS — Keep It Short and Simple. Keep this thought in mind throughout your letter-writing activities.

Effective letters come from:
- prior planning — thinking before you write
- a clear writing style — concise and simple
- good presentation — already dealt with.

Planning your letters

Many of the faults of ineffective, sloppy, letters can be

laid at the door of insufficient (or non-existent) prior thought.

Before you start to write a business (or any other, for that matter) letter, you should determine:

- **why** you need to write — your purpose
- **who** you are writing to — the reader, and
- **what** you have to put across — the content

Figure 7.1 illustrates the relationship between these three basic questions and the end result.

There has to be a purpose — a **why** — for every letter. Too often, a business letter does not make clear its reason for existence. Yet the objective of most business letters is straightforward. It is either: to persuade someone (to buy something, or to agree to a course of action); or it is to inform someone (of a result, etc.). And sometimes the purpose is both.

The aim of a sales letter — such as the one shown in Chapter 6 — is to *persuade* the recipient to buy your product or service. If you are writing to a client to say that you cannot deliver on time, you are *informing* — but you are also hoping to *persuade* the client against taking adverse action.

Before you start out to write a letter, think about why you need to write it. For a while, make a practice of writing that purpose on a piece of paper — and having it in front of you while writing. You need to keep your objective clearly in mind throughout — it will ensure that your writing is properly directed. A letter without a well-defined purpose is like a ship without a destination: merely travelling hopefully.

The purpose determined, think next of the recipient of your letter — the **who**.

You would write one type of letter to a colleague with expertise in the same business as yourself; you would write a completely different letter to eg, a child. That is obvious. But it is often overlooked when writing to a

Figure 7.1 *The three basic questions relating to writing a letter — and the result.*

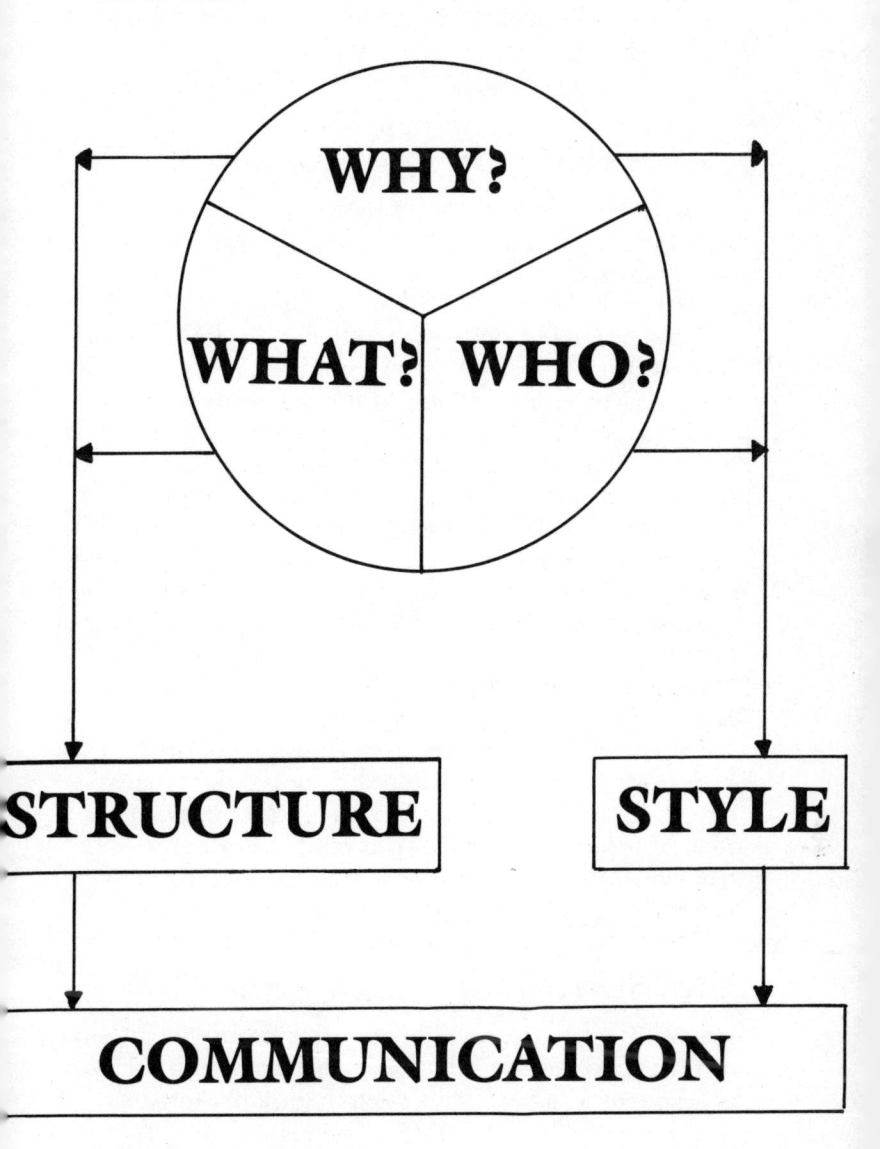

business contact, say, whose area of expertise is different from your own. It is too easy to assume that your reader will *automatically* understand what you are writing. Without thought on your part, sometimes they will not.

The first (and second, and third,) rule of effective letter writing is therefore:

* THINK ABOUT THE NEEDS OF THE READER *

Think always, "Will Mr Smith understand that, or should I write it more simply?" The answer will almost always be to simplify.

It is worth thinking too, about the possibility of your letter being passed on to someone else in the receiving organisation. You may be writing to a colleague with the same expertise as yourself; but the colleague may have to pass on your letter to, say, an accountant, for approval. Will the accountant understand your jargon? So . . . think about the possibility of there being a "secondary reader", and allow for this.

The next thing is to make sure that you really know **what** you are going to say (write). Which of us has not written a letter, signed it and posted it . . . and only then remembered that an important point has been omitted? That will not happen if you plan your letters before you write them.

If the letter is particularly important — and when you are starting up your own mini-business, which letter is not? — it is worth listing the points to be made on a sheet of scrap paper. From this list, you can go on to determine a structure for your letter.

A letter structure

The basic structure suitable for virtually any business letter is relatively simple. (Even simpler than the HIBA structure of a sales letter.) A letter should consist of:

- a beginning
- a middle
- an end

Think about the arrival of your letter. It often comes "out of the blue". It may be quite unexpected. Immediately therefore, you the writer, must tell the reader why you are writing and what about. That is the function of the beginning.

A typical *beginning* might therefore say something like:

I am writing to ask for your assistance. I have been commissioned by XXY Co Ltd to produce a report for them on . . . I believe you may be able to help me with . . .
or:
Thank you for your enquiry, dated 25 December, about my office services. I can offer a variety of typing and other services and I enclose a brochure outlining these.

In both cases, the beginning quickly makes it clear to the reader what the letter is all about — its purpose. In the first example, the writer explains immediately that he/she is seeking assistance. In the second, it is immediately made clear that the letter is in response to the reader's own enquiry — and this is given a date for speed of reference. (We all get letters which refer to "Your recent letter" — which usually means it was a month or so ago.)

It will sometimes be worth explaining the purpose of the letter quite specifically: "The purpose of this letter is to . . ."

In business correspondence there is also much advantage in giving a letter a title. When replying to a letter which itself has a title, you should of course repeat the same title in your letter. If you are initiating the correspondence and can choose your own title, make it as specific as possible — ie, helpful. A title helps to switch the reader's mind away from its current concern and onto *your* subject.

The middle of a straightforward letter is the "meat" of the letter. This is where you make your case, outline the facts, or pose your questions.

You have already — to avoid omitting anything — listed all the points you wish to include in the letter. You have also identified your purpose. Now put those two considerations together.

Arrange the points in the case, the facts, in a logical sequence that will best achieve your purpose. Make sure that, to you, all the points are important; alternatively, if you may not be able to include everything in the letter, sort the points, facts or questions into degrees of importance (ie, assistance in achieving the purpose) — into "musts, needs and wants":

1 . . . must include (to achieve the purpose)
2 . . . need to include
3 . . . want to include

We have already discussed (Chapter 5) the desirability of restricting a business letter to a single page. This will not always be possible, but two-page letters should be the exception, not the rule; they should be reserved for particularly complex topics.

Within the limitations therefore, of a reasonable overall length for your letter, bring in all the "musts" and as many of the "needs" as you can. And maybe you can include the odd "want" — an example perhaps, to leaven the lump of "essentials". But don't include more points than are necessary for the letter to achieve its objective.

You should also, at this stage, make sure that you yourself really *understand* what you are going to write. There is nothing like having to explain something simply, to identify one's own shortcomings. If you don't know, you can't explain.

The main content taken care of, you now need to finish the letter, to round it off. There is one school of thought that suggests that once you have said it all you should just stop. Maybe, but that can look rather ragged. Far better to end the letter with a specific point.

You can, with advantage, use the final paragraph of a letter to:

- advise that you will ring on a specific date, to discuss the letter content; or
- advise the date you can deliver by, or by when you are seeking a reply to your questions; or
- briefly summarise the major points contained in a long letter; or, at the very least,
- "look forward to hearing from you".

Clear simple writing

Now that you have worked out, in detail, what you are going to write, in what order, and for what purpose, you are ready to think about the actual writing — the stringing together of the words. And, as we have already noted, your writing needs to be a model of clarity.

You can go a long way towards achieving clarity by thinking back to what we described as the first (second and third) rule of effective letter writing: thinking about the needs of the reader. What does the reader need?

The reader of a business letter wants to be able to absorb the content quickly and easily. A busy businessperson will not want to waste time puzzling out what you mean, nor ploughing through an unnecessarily long, over-wordy letter. We have already mentioned how those requirements can be met, by following the KISS rule — by Keeping It (your writing) Short and Simple.

Let's consider how best to apply these concepts in practice.

The first principle of effective writing — and of the KISS rule — is to keep it short. Not just the overall length, which we have already discussed, but within the

letter too. "Short writing" is, by its very nature almost inevitably, simple and easy to understand. In a nutshell, "short writing" means using:
- short words
- short sentences
- short paragraphs

Short words are "easy words". If, when reading, you meet a word you don't understand, your first reaction is to hope that its meaning will come clear from the context. If it doesn't, you hope your lack of understanding won't matter; and you skip it. As a last resort you consult the dictionary. And you curse the writer. If that happens often, and your reading is not essential, you will give up. Almost always, the word you get stuck on, is a long one.

Now apply that reaction, in reverse, to your own writing. You have no captive readership; your reader can always give up. So, don't use words that your reader will not immediately understand. And the best way of meeting that requirement is to use short, "everyday" words.

Try to avoid words of more than three syllables; you can often convey a meaning better by using two or three shorter words in place of one long one. (In counting the syllables though, ignore the "add-ons": ignore *dis-, un-, -ly, -ing,* and the like. These do not make a simple everyday word difficult.)

At the end of the day though, if the long word is the *only* correct one, use it. But try to find a way to make its meaning clear to the reader.

Short sentences too, are generally easy to understand. There is of course, nothing fundamentally wrong with a long sentence — many literary giants use them extensively. But it is difficult to write an easy-to-understand long sentence. It takes a lot of writing skill. A short sentence though is (relatively) easy to write — and hard to make incomprehensible. There is little scope for confusion in a short sentence. (Notice how, having used what some may consider a longish word, I explain it — but tactfully.) So, take the easy course: write in short sentences.

To quantify that recommendation, I suggest working to an average "sentence" length of 15 or 16 words; stick as rigidly as possible to a maximum sentence length of 25 words. For the purpose of this "rule", treat a semi-colon or a colon as the equivalent of a full-stop. (Thus, I count the first sentence in this paragraph as two "sentences": of 17 and 13 words length, respectively.)

Having accepted these sentence-length criteria, look at your own writing.

For a while, until "short writing" becomes second nature, you should actually count the words in each sentence you write. You are likely to find many sentences that extend to well over thirty words. This is not at all unusual. Many business letter writers seem to ramble on at great length.

Now look at those longer sentences in more detail. The chances are that there is a mid-sentence "and", that could well be replaced with a full-stop. Make that change — and see how much better the sentences read.

Watch out too, whenever you contemplate adding in a qualifying phrase. Who has not drafted a letter, read it through, decided further qualification was needed . . . and inserted something — often between dashes — in mid-sentence? (Like that.) It is usually better to rewrite the original sentence completely. Maybe it should now be two sentences.

The use of short sentences automatically simplifies your punctuation too.

A short sentence can seldom accommodate more than just a full-stop and an occasional comma. And, while I am using colons and semi-colons in writing this book, they are often best avoided in business letters. Use them only when you have full confidence in your writing skills.

Be careful in following my suggestion of short sentences though. I am not recommending a *uniformity* of sentence length. Aim at the 15-16 word average length; but don't make all sentences the same length. You can achieve the 15-16 word average whilst varying the sentence lengths. And this you should do.

(Remember though that, if you are to maintain a 15-word average, for each long, 25-word sentence, you need a 5-word balancing sentence. Like this one.)

If all your sentences are of a similar length, your writing will be boring and perhaps staccato. But if you intersperse very short and relatively long sentences with average length ones, the overall effect will be "an easy read". Notice how I vary my sentence lengths throughout this book. (And yes, I know, I occasionally exceed my own 25-word limit. These recommendations are meant to be broken; they are advice, not rules carved on tablets of stone.)

Without doubt, the use of short words and short sentences will make your writing more "readable". There is no need to consider using any of the popular readability checks: the Fog Index, etc. The short words and the recommended average sentence-lengths will automatically lead to commendably low indices (ie easy readability).

Short paragraphs like short sentences, will ease the task of the reader. As Fowler explains, (in *Modern English Usage*) the purpose of a fresh paragraph is to give the reader a rest, a chance to pause and ensure that he/she has absorbed what has gone before. At the same time, an over-long paragraph *looks* like hard work. And the *appearance* of paragraphs is the main justification for the recommended shortness.

Fowler also explains rather well the logic of paragraph content. Each paragraph should contain an homogenous unit of thought; if the result of this is a paragraph which *appears* too long, it may be sub-divided. Conversely though, two independent thoughts should never be combined in one paragraph, even if the result of this separation is an unduly short paragraph.

It is less realistic to recommend word-lengths for paragraphs than it is for sentences; much will depend on the writer's judgement of the overall appearance — and on the length of the line. (A six- or seven-line typed paragraph may look about right — and contain about 60 words. The same number of words printed in a narrow newspaper column might look quite long. This would depend on the "quality" of the newspaper.) That said, a 70-word, 7-8 line paragraph is a reasonable average to aim at in a typed business letter; a sensible maximum would be about twice that length. And an occasional single-sentence, very short, paragraph has a lot of impact too.

From an appearance point of view, paragraph lengths should of course be varied. Intersperse longish paragraphs with the occasional short one — and vice versa.

In a sales letter, as considered in Chapter 6, the above paragraph-length recommendations would not apply. In such letters, even shorter paragraphs should be the rule.

Writing that sounds right

Having achieved a short simplicity, you now need to make your writing read smoothly — to join the *RIGHT* words together.

A leading American *guru* on management communication skills, Robert Gunning, recommends that you:

WRITE AS YOU TALK

— which is a fine, concise way of putting it; but it needs amplification. The trouble is, too many of us don't actually talk very well. We want our writing to be better than that. So, what Gunning really means is,

Don't write anything that would sound uncomfortable, if spoken, rather than written.

(And when one sees what a long "rule" that becomes when more explicit, one can understand why Gunning put it so bluntly.) But the principle is correct. The nearer your written expression is to the way you speak, the more readily will it be understood.

For an initial period, having acknowledged that perhaps your writing needs some improvement, there is much merit in reading your draft letters aloud, to yourself. And this must actually be aloud, not just muttering under your breath. The object is for the words to go out of your mouth and re-enter your consciousness through your ears. The use of a second sense seems to make a difference.

As you read your work aloud, you will stumble over the occasional pompous phrase; something perhaps that you thought looked "correct" in a letter — but which sounds awkward when spoken aloud. (We all do it. It's good to get such phrases out of your system; just make sure you get them out of your letters too.) As a general rule, beware "correct" phraseology; usually, it's stilted.

Reading aloud will also do wonders for your punctuation. While reading, pause only when there is a full-stop or comma. The likelihood of imminent asphyxiation will quickly bring home to you the benefits of short sentences.

There are other ways in which your writing can be improved; but they are less susceptible to positive general advice. They are best expressed just as a list of "ways to improve".

- check your writing to make sure that your tenses are consistent. It is all too easy to start in the past tense and end in the present. Similarly, watch out for changing from first to third person. (I had to be careful with the person a few paragraphs above, moving from "you" to "one". But I think I got it right.)

- try to use the active voice rather than the passive — it sounds more positive. (The active voice says, "I did this." The passive voice says, "This was done.") Yet much business correspondence seems to make a virtue out of using the passive voice.

- check that each of your sentences has the necessary subject, object and verb. There should be no problems with short sentences, but you often find long sentences where the verb is lost among the qualifications and sub-clauses.

- avoid the use of foreign language phrases. Far better to say "From the start" than to hide your real meaning by writing *ab initio*. Such Latin "tags" are only used to impress the reader with the writer's supposed superiority; there is seldom a need for them. (*See* later, on impressing.)

- avoid qualifying the ultimate. You can no more be "very unique", or "absolutely dead", than you can be "slightly pregnant". You either is or you isn't.

- try to avoid — note my caution here — the use of the word "very". There is almost always a better way —ie, with a single, correct word — of expressing a thought than "very . . ." If something is "very thin", why not quantify the thinness? If "very good", is it not "excellent"?

- avoid exaggeration. Remember that the written word is a permanent record. You may sometimes exaggerate when speaking — your tone of voice and your expression will make it clear that you are exaggerating; when writing, there is no way of qualifying a statement, other than in further, associated writing.

You should also work to make your writing "flow" smoothly. The use of short words, short sentences and short paragraphs can, if not watched, lead to staccatto, disjointed writing; this may be clear, but it is no pleasure to read. It will not be an "easy read". To make your writing flow, look to your paragraphs.

Try to start each paragraph with a key thought; then expand and elaborate on this thought in the remainder of the paragraph. This sets the scene for the reader and makes the paragraph easier to understand.

Another way of making the reading flow more easily is to link successive paragraphs together. Make it clear to the reader that not every fresh paragraph is a wholly fresh thought; often it is one which follows from, and is linked in logic to, its predecessor.

Notice how the previous paragraph was subtly linked to its predecessor by the opening word, "another". As soon as the reader sees that word, he/she knows that the discussion is continuing, although on a slightly fresh tack.

The words "and" or "but" are another good simple way of linking paragraphs. Don't be put off by out-dated pedantic rules that prohibit starting sentences (or paragraphs) with "and" or "but". Many literary "greats" do it. So can you. The linkage improves the "flow".

Polishing

Your writing is now clear and simple; it sounds good when read aloud; and the whole "flows" as an integrated case. You are nearly there. All that is left to do is to give your writing a bit of a shine.

Having drafted a letter you should *always* read it through before typing (or printing, if using a word processor). You will probably not persist in reading aloud; this is good practice when learning, but time-consuming when busy working. So read through your writing to yourself, and *polish* it.

Polishing means weeding out the unreadable phrases and the pomposities. (With practice, you can identify these without the reading actually being aloud.) Polishing means cutting out the waffle too, all the over-writing. All of us use too many words; better letter-writers prune their drafts harshly. If you can cut out about ten per cent from the first draft of a letter, the result will be much improved.

Be unimpressive

And finally, in this section on improving letter-writing style, think back to the beginning of the chapter; we identified the importance of the reader.

The purpose of any business letter is to communicate your ideas, your wishes, your hopes, to that reader. The less the way in which the letter is written is actually noticed, the better the letter is. An obtrusive, noticeable style will hinder the communication process. That is why, we have aimed, throughout this chapter, at recommending the simplest, clearest writing style; one that will not hinder the understanding of the basic message.

It follows therefore that nothing you write should be such as to impress the reader with the supposed superiority or cleverness of the writer.

The corollary of the first (second and third) basic rule of effective letter writing is therefore:

NEVER TRY TO IMPRESS YOUR READER – JUST COMMUNICATE.

CASE STUDY – *Gordon*

Gordon — that's me — started building up his mini-business about forty years ago, writing magazine articles and books in his spare time. When he started up, he had no thoughts of such things as business plans or the like. He just wanted to write — and get paid for it. And, over the years, he built up a reasonable proficiency at the business.

A couple of years ago, Gordon reached the age (60) at which he could — but didn't have to — retire from his civil service job. He calculated that he would be able to earn enough from his writing — and other associated — activities, to supplement his pension sufficiently. He took the plunge.

Now, after eighteen months as a full-time writer, working as a mini-business, things are looking good. he has so far managed to get enough commissions for new non-fiction books to keep him very fully occupied . . . and there are other, spin-off, activities.

Because Gordon effectively started up his mini-business many years before, there were no new start-up expenses. He is well equipped with an Amstrad PC 1512 computer and a Star NB24-10 24-pin printer — and of course, a telephone. So far, a telephone answering machine has not proved necesssary —either he or his wife are always around — and, because there is a coin-operated photocopier in the local library, a copier is also unnecessary.

Were he to start from scratch, the cost of equipment alone would be around £1500 — the reference books and the contents of his filing cabinets would cost a lot more. He works in an "almost dedicated" room — a study — with the walls lined with reference and other books.

Before he retired, Gordon commuted to work in London; he was out of the house from 7.00 am till 7.00 pm. His writing had to be fitted in each evening between 8.00 and 9.00 pm and for about eight hours spread over the weekend. As a full-time writer he now works from 8.30 am till about 5.30 pm every day —and only slightly shorter hours on Saturdays and Sundays — when he is not working away from home. (Lecturing and recruitment interviewing take up about two days a week on average.)

All this work is paying off. At present his earnings, solely from writing (ie excluding anything from lecturing or interviewing) are now well over £5,000 a year and rising.

He does not use an accountant but his mini-business accounts are prepared for him by his bank, together with other financial matters. He is not registered for VAT.

His advice to those about to start up in the writing field is:

- build up your skills by working in your spare time before going full-time — the road to writing success is littered with many rejections;

- don't buy more than the most basic equipment until you earn enough to pay for it out of income;
- before offering written material to editors or publishers, study the market, and offer what they want;
- be business-like in all things — keep filing and accounts up-to-date and write "professional-looking" letters;
- and find some extra means of financial support — very few writers make a good living from writing along.

8
SELLING FACE TO FACE

No matter how effective your letters may be, few businesses can operate entirely by mail. You will almost certainly have to get out and meet your customers and clients. You will have to *sell* yourself and your product — face to face. And you're nervous about this prospect.

So is everyone else when they start. Even the much-travelled hard-bitten sales representative had to start sometime. And then, he or she was just as nervous as you are now. Sales reps overcome their fears; so can you. You're as capable as the average sales person, aren't you?

All you need is confidence. With confidence, you will *know* that you can make a good job of a face to face sales interview. Confidence will overcome your nervousness. And you can give yourself this confidence.

Confidence comes from having:

- a good presence
- a good product
- a good presentation

Your "presence", is a combination of how you look and how you behave. The "product" can be a thing — or a service. And the "presentation" is the *way* in which you put across your case.

Good presence

If you were able to place an order with one of two competitors whose products were absolutely equal, who

153

would you favour? (And yes, I know that absolute equality is an impossibility.) You would opt for the supplier who makes the best impression; the one you "like the look of".

In business, there can be few more apt sayings than the home-spun philosophy of the Christmas cracker's: "you never get a second chance to make a first impression." You *must* create a good impression — immediately.

We have already, in Chapter 5, stressed the importance of looking good. Particularly when you are on a selling expedition, your clothes — and your whole appearance — are an important part of your minibusiness. But there will be some occasions when you need to do more than just "look good". Maybe you feel that you look too old for the part — or, just as likely, too young.

Your feelings are wrong; age is less important than people think. *Attitude* and *liveliness* are far more important. But if your age contributes to your lack of confidence, it is worth doing something about. You can camouflage your age.

If you are worried that you are, or just look, too old, you can:

- wear more stylish clothes — but avoid being too trendy;
- adopt a modern hair style (even adding a hair piece if you're really worried about it);

but, most important of all . . .

- act and move energetically — in a nutshell, *think young.*

If you believe that you look too young for your own good, you can:

- dress more conservatively than your peers;

- keep your hair well-trimmed — avoid long hair (equally applicable to men or women);
- use *quality* accessories — brief-case, pen, etc. — they attract complimentary notice.

And, above all:

- DON'T SLUMP.

But there are other aspects of your appearance that affect the first impression you create. Take note of the impressions that may be conveyed by:

- your facial expression
- your body movements
- your tone of voice
- what you are actually saying

If you smile, you will at least look pleasant. Be careful that you don't smile too much though. Cheshire Cats make few sales. And there is evidence that the more senior a business person is, the less that person is likely to smile. (Maybe they get sour as they age?)

More important almost than thinking about smiling — the need for which is already widely recognised — is the need to look keen and alert. At all costs you should avoid a blank expression.

And, of course, look your customer straight in the eye. Make eye contact. An unwillingness to make eye contact can appear shifty. (And if you really can't bring yourself to look the customer straight in the eye, look at his forehead or her nose — or vice versa. The difference in eye-line will barely be noticeable.

Facial impression leads us nicely on to overall body language. The way you position yourself, the way you hold and move your body, every move you make, can help to generate an impression. Make sure it's a good one.

As we have already implied, slumping in your chair creates an adverse impression — an impression of degeneracy; "sitting tall" and leaning forward have the reverse effect — these give the impression of keenness. (But be careful: excessive leaning forward can be interpreted as aggressive — an attempt to violate another's "personal space". Well, no one said that body language was easy.)

Hiding your mouth behind your hand is another bad indicator: you don't wish people to know that it is you uttering those words — there's something wrong with them. (If you have halitosis, take breath-fresheners. Hiding behind your hand doesn't help.)

Even the way you introduce yourself can say something about you. Ideally, you should come forward willingly, prepared to shake hands. Hand-shaking is necessary body language; a welcoming and friendly gesture expected in business. Restrict your physical contact to the hand-shake though: some nationalities go in for a further simultaneous grip — on the shoulder perhaps — with the other hand; this is frowned upon in Britain. Make the hand-shake firm — beware the "wet fish shake" or the "limp wrist" — but do not prolong it.

If you have a business card — see Chapter 5 — give it to your potential customer immediately before or after you shake hands. It lets the person you are visiting remember your name — without straining the memory. And you want your name to be remembered. You may not get an order today — but there is always a next time.

So far, we have not thought about what you are going to say, or how you are going to say it. Without doubt, you should speak positively and without hesitation. Your voice should not be too quiet. Save the deliberately hushed voice for when you want to appear confidential, or to hold an already riveted listener.

As long as your voice is clear though, what you say is more important than the tone of your voice. Which brings us round to knowing what to say. And to get that right, you must prepare.

Good product

You have faith in your product — the goods or services you wish to sell. That's essential. But faith alone is not enough. You must also have all the facts, at your fingertips. You have just a few minutes in which to sell yourself; your client's attention span is short. (Who has not said to themselves, with feeling, "If only he would get to the point."?) You have to convince the customer that your product or service is necessary — and right — and do it quickly.

So . . . you must plan in advance how the sales interview is to go. For this, the HIBA approach which we met when looking at a sales letter in Chapter 6, is again valid. The plan for your sales interview should consist of:

H — **the hook.** Very quickly, you have to interest, and then hold the attention of, the customer.
I — **the information.** You must "set out your market stall" very quickly, explaining just what is on offer.
B — **the benefits.** You must demonstrate to your customer, while you still have his or her attention, just "what's in it for him — or her".
A — **the action.** Now you must get the order. Everything before this has been hypothetical; getting the order is *real,* this is "crunch time".

And, you must do all of this in a short space of time. Try to get it all across within five minutes, start to finish. If the client/customer wants to take more time, that's his/her perogative; your aim must be to complete in five minutes, to avoid any accusation of time-wasting.

The hook is of great importance. Yet, too often, the advice on how to interest a client suggests an over-brash, over-pushy, approach which could well be counter-productive. Too often, the text-book advice on the hook sounds like a manual for door-step evangelists. And we all know the response they get.

With some customers, and with some products, it is right to ask a question with which it would be perverse to disagree. "Could you use a better quality product — at the same price as you are already paying?"

I do not believe though that I would get very far in selling my one-day writing courses if I asked a potential client, "Would you like all of your staff to be good letter-writers?" I think I might achieve more success if I rephrased it, "I'll bet you wish some of your staff were better at letter-writing." And maybe I'd do better still if I briefly outlined my views about literary ability at work — and how it can be improved.

This latter approach might work best, because I know that many employers are unhappy about the writing skills of their staff. I would be preaching to the converted; telling them what they want to hear.

You must work out for yourself the type of hook most likely to be suitable for each occasion. Your judgement will be influenced not only by the type of client or customer, but also of course, by the product or service you are selling. Make your judgement *in advance*, before you enter the lion's den. Then you're ready to start pitching straight away. But . . . be prepared to switch tracks if you find that your predetermined approach is not right. (Watch out for eyes glazing over.)

Once the listener is hooked, you can expand — elaborate on what you have to sell.

One sure-fire way of "displaying your wares" — of telling the client or customer what you have to offer —is to adopt an approach much favoured by labour organisers of old. the old factory gate union men adopted a standard approach for their harangues. They used to, "Tell 'em what they were going to say, tell 'em . . . and then tell 'em what they've told 'em."

Think of this approach as the "three times" (3x) rule.

It works as well in a face-to-face interview today, as it ever did outside the factory gate. (We shall meet the same approach again in the next chapter; it is equally valid if you need to give a talk to a group of people.)

If I were adopting this approach to sell my one-day lectures I would structure my statement to the client by the 3x rule:

1 "Let me tell you about my own package of one-day lectures: I can offer you a course on writing and another on speaking. They are both really concentrated instruction sessions. There is no padding; the whole of the time is used constructively." (Remember, I've already used the *hook* to gain the client's interest.)

2 "There are two one-day courses. The writing course consists of three lectures — one each on planning, writing, and presentation — and then a practical workshop session; 'students' are given an everyday topic to write about briefly, then their work is constructively criticised."

   "The speaking course also has three lectures — planning, note-making and delivery — and a workshop session; 'students' are given time to prepare a short talk which they then deliver — and get instant helpful criticism. For each course, fully comprehensive hand-outs are provided."

3 "So you see, I am offering two very concentrated and practical courses on the most important communications skills — writing and speaking. The courses are run at your own offices, so there's no waste of staff time. And they cost only £000 per day. Without doubt, they are better value than anything else available."

And already, in the third part of this 3x approach, you can see that I am beginning to outline the *benefits* to the client. Now I must work on this a little more.

159

It would be useful if I could truly personalise the benefits of my courses to the client. To do this though, I would need to know how many of their staff need communication training. (And although some of the senior staff may *need* it, they may not be prepared to acknowledge the need). In discussion though, it might have been possible to get some idea of how many staff they have. I can then quickly do some calculations — on the basis of 12 "students" per course — and tell them what a package of say four pairs of courses will cost, perhaps offering a slight discount.

The final task is to get a committment, a sale. Everything leading up to this has been largely hypothetical; now you want the client to say YES. You've got to the *action* stage. You may discover that the person to whom you have been speaking doesn't have the authority to commit that much money. Ideally, you should have discovered that earlier — but it's not always that easy. (Maybe though, you can get a smaller financial commitment: for the organisation to take four courses. If so, grab that partial success like a shot. You can always hope to come back for more).

Maybe, you have convinced your contact person of the need for, and suitability of, whatever it is you are offering, but the final authority to place a firm order is missing. You could offer to "help" your contact in selling you to the person with that extra authority. Two of you will probably do it better than one alone — particularly if you are the extra person.

Good presentation

We have already begun to expand on how you present your case. The 3x rule is as much about presentation as it is about structure and content. But there are other points to bear in mind as you present your case to the customer/client. And these are best listed:

- Many beginner sales-people qualify what they say; you must be more positive. Beginners tend to say things like, "you may not (initially) agree, but . . .", which invites disagreement; or even the uncertain, "Isn't that so?" Both of these phrases suggest a lack of conviction. Try saying, instead, "You must agree that . . ." or "I'm sure that you'll agree . . ." or just, "This is so." Be positive.
- When you can't be too positive — for fear of appearing over-pushy (there are such situations, but fewer than you think) — and you have to qualify your statements, do it in a strong and positive way. Maintain eye-contact, don't avert your gaze, or lower your voice deferentially. (If you do either of these things, you're dead. You will have lost the "high ground" of the client's interest.) Make a clear statement.
- Try to have something to *give* — not just show — the person you are interviewing: a small sample of your product (a sprat to catch a mackerel); an example of a brochure, photograph, or whatever, prepared for a previous client/customer; a leaflet describing your previous books; even just a typical handout sheet for your lectures.

  There was much truth in the old saying that "you have to speculate to accumulate". Be prepared to give something away. Anything (good) that you can give a client to look at, or handle, while you are talking is as useful as a visual aid to a public speaker — *see* next Chapter.
- Avoid "knocking" your competitors — or at least,. don't do it too obviously. If it comes up, you might try saying something like, "I realise that there are other firms offering . . . that have some similarities. But really, they are in a different ball-game altogether. My . . . is a far superior product, not comparable with theirs in any way. There's room for both of us — we

are at opposite ends of the market. And yet my prices are virtually the same as theirs."

With luck — and further persuasive chatter from you — that approach will reduce the risks of comparison with your competitors.

- Be prepared to combat negative *vibes* immediately you sense them. However a "no" is wrapped up, it's still a "no", and must be dealt with quickly, on the spot. Find out *why* you are getting the negative feed-back; try to bring the reason "out into the open". Once you know what the trouble is, acknowledge that the client has a good reason to be suspicious or unwilling, or whatever. And then do your very best to refute the argument.

  (Even if the client/customer's objections are illogical, it still pays to take them on board. Anyway, a weak case should be far easier to shoot down than a valid one. And acknowledging a customer's fears is more likely to get them "on your side" than if you just dismiss their worries as nonsense.)

  However you do it though, you must always demolish the objections. If you can't do this, more often than not, you should probably give up the mini-business, and go back to being a wage-slave. Being "in business" means selling.

- Be very careful how you address people. It is potentially sexist to address all men as "Mr", and all women by their first names, or vice versa; this is an implied discrimination (but in which direction, I'm not sure).

  Be careful too about using abbreviations or expected nicknames. If someone is introduced to you as William Smith, this probably means he doesn't like being called Bill, or Willie — even by his friends. Similarly Deborah Digby probably *hates* being called Debbie or "Debs".

- Make sure that you pay full attention to *all* that the client or customer says in your presence. The client may not want what you are offering — but be urgently seeking some service of which you are equally capable, but hadn't thought to offer.

    (I was talking to a potential client about my courses in business letter writing, when he casually asked whether I could help in running a graduate recruitment campaign for him. This was an area of freelance work I had not then envisaged. Momentarily, I was "thrown"; I recovered though, thought quickly about it, and said yes. That gave me ten days of fascinating work that year — and I now hope for more work of a similar nature.)

- Before a face-to-face interview closes, you should summarise the results and agreements reached: a decision to purchase or an order for so many products, or an agreement that you will deliver specific material at a specified time.

    But that alone is not enough. Be really efficient. As soon as you get home, write a brief letter confirming all that has been decided. Your client/customer can hardly fail to be impressed by this efficiency — larger firms take an age to produce such simple letters. And you will have got your confirmation onto the client's desk before the details have been forgotten.

That's selling. That's good business.

CASE STUDY – *Barbara*

Barbara is a freelance writer. But she also makes craft jewellery, operating as a sole trader. Her mini-business of jewellery-making is not a full-time occupation; but nor is her writing. Taken together though, they occupy just about all her available time. And together, they are her main means of financial support.

Barbara started her craft jewellery mini-business about ten years ago, in her forties. Initially, it was a spare-time occupation — something to do, apart from raising a family. It was stimulating and it was fun. But then, after her divorce in the early eighties, the work took off — to meet the financial needs of her situation. Nowadays, she says, "The business is as successful as I need it to be. But the craft scene is getting more and more competitive these days."

She does not work regular hours at making her jewellery, nor has she ever needed to do so. The work depends on the demand, which is seasonal. It tends to be a very full-time job in the three months run-up to Christmas. When the demand is heavy, she works "round the clock" to meet it; she has learnt her lesson well, that a self-employed person is chiefly free to work execessively hard — or go under. In the slack season, she has more time for her writing.

Her writing has spin-off benefits for her jewellery making too. Barbara has written several articles about her jewellery-making and about herself — she was even sponsored to make a short film about her work.

She does not rely solely on her articles (or the film) to bring in more business though. She sells from home, as a result of personal recommendations; she sets out her wares and sells from trestle-table stalls at better craft fairs within a reasonable radius of home; and she sells wholesale to one or two large organisations — and to a few selected shops and craft outlets.

Barbara advertises occasionally in local newspapers, and also gets a lot of editorial coverage. And she gives talks about her craft to schools, WI groups and the like. ("A thirty minute talk to a handful of WI members in a village hall, can yield more revenue than all three days at a rain-drenched County Show.")

Working on small items of jewellery, Barbara has not needed much in the way of a workshop or equipment. Her start-up costs were small; she borrowed a small sum from a friendly relation; she had no need to prepare a formal business plan. Since then, the craft jewellery mini-business has built up slowly but steadily. Barbara now earns several thousand pounds a year from it; this, together with her writing income, suffices. And, very sensibly, she is buying a tax-efficient self-employed pension out of her earnings.

She works, she says, "out of a dedicated cupboard and a few odd corners". Office equipment is minimal and, of course, multi-purpose: whatever she needs for the mini-business, she also needs for her freelance writing — and vice versa. Basically she relies on a telephone with answering machine, and an "Amstrad".

Given her time over again, Barbara would start up a similar mini-business. She is totally "sold" on the self-employed way of life. "You are doing what you enjoy doing; you stand or fall by your own success or failure; and your're answerable to no-one but yourself. It's a great life."

Her advice to those about to set up their own mini-business is:

- remember that your income will fluctuate. ("One week you'll be awash with tenners, the next, struggling to find a fiver to pay the milkman.")
- remember that if you take a holiday, you lose income.
- get a good accountant.

9
MAKING A PRESENTATION

We have discussed the problems of face to face selling on an individual basis. There will be times though, when you are required to "make a presentation" of your product or service to a larger group — a committee, perhaps. Similarly, it can often be productive — at least, in the longer run — to give a talk about your product or service to a social group or professional organisation.

Local Women's Institutes, Townswomens' Guilds, Rotary or Lions clubs and Round Tables alike, are all on the lookout for potential speakers. And I differentiate quite specifically now between a lunch-time talk, which can be direct and fairly low-key technical, and an after-dinner speech, which has to be much more polished and perhaps even witty. A lunch-time talk is relatively easy to do. From a simple lunch-time talk, big orders can sometimes follow. You never know.

So, it is useful to be capable of giving a short, not-too-technical talk about what you do.

And I wager that the mere mention of giving a talk has already made you nervous. This is understandable. But you can conquer these fears. Once again, it comes down to building up your confidence.

As with face to face selling, confidence in your ability to give a talk will come from three things. You need:
- preliminary thinking
- preparation
- practice.

Let us look at these three stages and see how easy it really is.

Thinking about talking

If you are to make a success of giving a short talk, the prime requirement — too often ignored — is to think first. You need to determine the who, the what and the why of your talk. Who are you to talk to? What do you have to say? And why?

And because you are going to talk about your mini-business — let's face it, there's no other reason for you to stand up and talk — you already know what you are going to talk about. Basically, you're going to talk about yourself and what you do. So, you start off knowing at least a part of the what.

But back to the first of the questions you need to ask yourself. Who are you going to talk to? You need to know this, so that you can target your talk properly. It would clearly be wrong to think of offering the same talk to a group of primary school-children, to a meeting of the local WI, or to a local government committee contemplating employing your services. Their knowledge and their interests would vary widely.

You need to know, very broadly, the likely age of your audience, because this will affect the way you talk. And similarly, you need to know the likely level of knowledge of your audience. A talk on, say film processing, would need to be "slanted" differently for the WI, than for members of the local camera club.

Before you start to prepare your talk, you also need to think about how big the audience is likely to be. The way in which you put your material across will be very different if to a group of half-a-dozen business clients around a table, or to an audience of hundreds in a theatre. For a small audience your talk could perhaps be relatively informal — and allow for questions and other interruptions; for a large audience you must be more precise — and you need to retain *control*.

For a small group, your notes (see below) can perhaps

be minimal; for a big audience you will probably prefer to work from fuller notes.

Reverting to the what question, despite knowing that you intend to talk about yourself, and what you have to offer, you need to consider the content of your talk more specifically. You also need to ensure you have *enough* to say.

The why is often overlooked. Like letter-writing, there has to be a purpose. But with the type of talk we are considering, this is almost always to *persuade* — which embraces either instruction or selling. You are going to stand up and talk about yourself, or your product, or your craft or profession. Your purpose is either to teach the audience how to follow in your footsteps, or to interest them in buying your product or service.

You need to *know* your purpose before you start preparing your talk. The why will affect the way in which you put your message across.

So, before you start the detailed preparation of your material, ascertain the who, the what and the why. You should know, for example: that you are to talk to a group of half-a-dozen hard-nosed middle-aged men (all men?) who control the purchasing activities of an important company; they know precisely what they want, as an end product — but know (and care) little about your production problems; they are seeking only to decide on their next year's supplier. If you succeed in winning them over you can expect a big order.

Or maybe you are to talk for twenty minutes to your local WI, telling them about how you started making lace, how they can take it up as a hobby, and showing them examples of your work. Your object may be to get more people interested in lace-making, and to buy their material from you — and perhaps to sell them copies of your latest book "How to make lace".

Whatever your talk is to be, you must first be sure about the who, the what, and the why.

Preparing a talk

But knowing the who, what and why is only the start. After that, you have to gather your material together, decide how you will *structure* your talk, and prepare the notes from which you will speak.

Gathering material together: It is essential that you gather your material together — and make brief notes of all the facts and topics you want to include. Writing the facts and topics down allows you to consider their relevance. You can then categorise, and mark, each of the items by its importance in relation to your predetermined purpose. Mark the items "essential", "desirable", or "makeweight". (Or *musts, needs,* and *wants.*)

Now review the available material for quantity related to the time for which you have to speak. Think about whether there are enough, merely of the essential items, to fill the time. Maybe there is too much material: you will have to prune it down. If there is not enough, reckon on bringing in some of the "desirable" items.

Think too about the balance of interest in your essential items. Might it be better to include some of the less important, but perhaps more interesting or amusing, makeweight items — to "leaven the lump" of your talk? Too many facts can be very dull. An occasional anecdote does wonders — particularly if it is amusing.

It is often wise to limit the scope of your talk — to just one aspect of your work, service or product — in order to make a more positive impression. It is far better to put across a few points well, than drag out every item from an unsorted rag-bag.

Structuring a talk: An unstructured talk is unworthy of the name. But structuring is not difficult to do. A structure is merely a logical arrangement of the available material, the sequence in which the points are to be presented.

Some talks may reasonably be structured as a series of steps in an obvious direction: an example of this would be a description of a manufacturing process "First you do this, then that, then the other . . ." Others might follow an historical sequence.

Many talks though can readily be "adjusted" to fit a structure which is a development of the 3x approach mentioned in the previous chapter. It is generally recognised that an audience's ability to take in information is limited to just a few points. Three main points are about right. (But these three main points can be further sub-divided if necessary — ideally, again into three.) And, as we have already mentioned, major points are best repeated.

A useful structure for many talks is therefore the 3 x 3 rule. Arrange your talk material into three sections, three main points — and put these across three times to the audience.

Tell the audience that there are three main points, a, b and c; then go through these three items and elaborate on each of them — further sub-dividing into three again if necessary; then sum up; reminding the audience of the three points and their importance.

(If you think of the first part of the present chapter as being akin to a talk — on how to give a talk — you will notice that I am working to a basic 3 x 3 approach here. The chapter starts by identifying confidence as the prime requirement for a speaker.

Confidence comes from three things — thinking, preparation, and practice. Then I further sub-divide the prior thinking into three — who, what and why — and elaborate on each. At the end, I recapped on this too. I then moved on to the second of the initial three items, preparation — and have sub-divided that in turn, into three — gathering material, structuring the talk, and preparing notes from which to speak. And that's where we are now.)

Preparing your notes: Once you have gathered together all your information, and decided on a structure for the talk, you can prepare the notes from which you are to talk. These can come in different formats.

If you are making a sales presentation to a *small* group of business people, perhaps around a table, your notes should be relatively unobtrusive. In this situation, there is a lot to be said for a single sheet of A4 paper. If you are to stand up before a group audience or even a "class", I would recommend that your notes should be on a set of small cards. if you are "lumbered" with a talk to a large gathering, cards again or perhaps a set of half-A4 sheets — with the corners folded for ease of turning. (My own preference is always for small cards — like post cards.)

Whatever their format though, some sort of notes are virtually essential. But they must be just that — notes. You should never — unless you are giving an address to the United Nations or the like — write out, in full, what you intend to say.

Unless you are a trained thespian (or politician), reading a fully scripted talk will make you sound dull and lifeless. Notes though, *force* you to think on your feet, to put life into your talk. The only qualification I would make to that advice is that the notes for a large audience should be fuller, more complete, than the notes for a talk to a small group. And you might, perhaps, actually script your brief opening paragraph. (It's very important that you get the opening right.)

How comprehensive you make your notes is up to you. Remember though that you will wish to pick up the message from the card at a glance. You will not wish to stop speaking while you read a whole sentence to yourself; you just need the key word. As an example, I would expect to be able to put across the whole of the content of this paragraph from a note merely saying "glance — key words".

To talk about the previous paragraph, my note would say little more than "Script — dull. Notes *make* lively. Big group, fuller notes. Maybe script opening."

It makes good sense to number your cards and link them together; I use a 2-inch long Treasury tag through a hole in the top left corner of each card. (Short tags cause problems when turning over the cards; a longer tag makes turning easy.) The value of numbering and tagging is that you can almost instantly recover should you be so unfortunate as to drop your note-cards. Your note-cards are your crutches; they will ensure that you do not become tongue-tied. The knowledge that they will keep you going, helps give you the essential confidence.

A further advantage of talking from notes is that you can expand or contract your speaking to fit the time remaining.

Some speakers underline their notes in three different colours — representing *musts, needs,* and *wants:* they know that they have to include everything underlined in red; they add in as much as they find necessary of the items underlined in other colours. Other speakers have anecdotes, on separate cards, that they bring in when there is time and omit when there is not.

I favour the latter approach, if any. I do not find it easy to think about the significance of a colour coding when in mid-talk. In my view, speaking notes should be as simple and easy to understand as possible.

Practising your talk

Your notes complete, you are ready to give your talk. Well, not quite. Whether this is to be your first talk ever, or you have done so many that you are beginning to get *blasé* about them, it pays to have what is called a "stagger through". This is exactly what it sounds like. A dry run, a rehearsal.

My own practice is to take my notes, close my study door — and present my talk to myself, *aloud.* I try to say the sort of things I will say *on the night,* expanding sensibly from my notes; I try to make the gestures and pauses I will make when the real time comes. And I check my timing.

There can be few worse experiences than to sit through a speaker who goes on . . . and on . . . and on. You must make very sure that you are not one of those bores. (You will make few direct or spin-off sales if you are. And don't forget, that's the name of the game, the main reason you're giving the talk.)

You owe it to yourself, and to the all-important audience, to speak for your allotted time: no more, no less. Having a "stagger through" before you talk lets you check how long you are going to last out. You may need more material: it's better to discover that before, rather than after, you stand up. You may be likely to over-run: don't actually remove any material from your notes; just mark it with a coloured "flash", or bracket it — to leave out unless you need more.

You will find though, even with experience, that the timing of your "stagger through" will not be totally reliable.

I find I talk faster in real life than in any practice — despite numerous reminders to myself to slow down. (I tend to get carried away, and speed up.) You may be different. You may find that you slow down more than you expect. This is for you to discover. No matter how inaccurate a "stagger through" may be though, it is an invaluable necessity for any beginner — and for many reasonably-experienced speakers too.

What you actually say *on the night* though, will NOT be the same as what you said in your "stagger through". If you give the same talk half-a-dozen times, from the same set of notes, it will be different each time. It will contain all the same material, but the way you express this will vary. Because you are speaking from notes, rather than a script, it will be alive; you will speak with conviction and enthusiasm each time. But the "stagger through" will have helped you to gain that all-important confidence. You will *know* that you can put your message across; that you won't run dry; that you won't rabbit on. You will have "proved" your notes.

One final point about preparations: don't do it all too long in advance of the real occasion, or you will forget. If you feel you must prepare about a week before, (I get nervous if I have not done my preparation well in advance.) then have a further "stagger through" the day before the real event. That will bring it all back, fresh, into your memory again. But whatever you do, don't try to memorise what you are to say — it MUST come fresh.

And guard your note-cards as you would your life. In speaking terms, they are just that — your life. Without their support, in the theatrical sense, you could "die".

Delivering a talk

But now the actual day has come. Your first public speech — that's too grand a word, your first talk, your first presentation are better ways of thinking of it — is upon you.

First, let's just go back, momentarily, to the day before. It pays to telephone the organisers of the WI meeting, or the secretary of the business group, to confirm where you are to go and at what time, and who if anyone will meet you. You may already know, but "belt and braces" confirmation will help safeguard your fragile confidence.

On the day, arrive early. Find the room where you are to talk. Check that it is not a large barn devoid of any form of public address equipment. (And if you are going to be required to use a PA system, check that it works — before anyone else arrives.) You may have some say in how the room is arranged and where you stand. (I have, on more than one occasion, arrived cautiously early and then had to spend all the available time unstacking and arranging chairs. Better I did it myself, before the appointed time, than start the talk in an atmosphere of unfurnished chaos.)

If you are going to use visual aids (*See* below), check that the projector works; find out how it switches on and off; check that it is focussed; check that the screen is visible from all corners of the room.

And then, the meeting begins. If it is, say, a WI meeting, you may be on a platform, with a chairperson who will introduce you. (You should have provided them, well in advance, with suitable introductory material.) If it is a board meeting or the like, you may be called in from an ante-room — with virtually no time to "settle yourself" in the board room proper.

Set aside your fears. Of course you are nervous. You would be no good if you were not. (Brash over-confidence usually comes before a disastrous presentation.) The butterflies in your stomach are merely signs of the adrenalin working. Harness that adrenalin, ignore the flutters and pitch in. You know what you are going to say. Now say it.

Stand up. (Standing gives you a position of slight authority, which will boost your confidence.) If it's a big group, look at someone near the back — and talk to him. Don't shout, just *project* your voice. Speak clearly and — if possible — slowly. Your voice will go where your eyes go. You will be able to tell from that person's expression whether or not he can hear you. If necessary, raise your voice a little till he can.

Finish a sentence; then turn your head and look at someone else, and speak to her. Do not speak to just a single person all through the whole talk. Look at various people. Watch for their nods of approval (as long as they are not "nodding off"), and "feed them". Offer them more to agree with.

Identify the person most likely to chuckle at your (probably weak) puns — and address the next one directly at her. You need someone to spark off the audience's enthusiasm. A ready chuckler will often get them all going. And then they're "on your side".

While you are standing there giving your talk, try to to give some thought to how you look. (Yes, I know you are concentrating on what you are saying, but try.) Stand up, stand square, and stand still; don't wander around the platform — or your side of the table, if it's a small meeting. Avoid the habit of leaning on the lectern — it could collapse. Avoid too, leaning forward and embracing it confidentially.

Try not to waggle your hands around. Semaphore is only relevant if the audience are a long, long way away. Your note cards offer an extra bonus in this respect; they give you something to do with your hands. But a very occasional sweeping gesture can be worth making, to emphasise eg size. (Be careful there is no one in the path of your sweeping hands though. Giving the chairperson a black eye is not conducive to lasting popularity.)

If, like me, you wear glasses, try not to keep pushing them up on your nose — as, I'm afraid, I habitually do. Resist too, the temptation to remove them and wave them in the air, to emphasise a point. Both are merely nervous habits — best broken.

If a man, resist the temptation to jiggle the coins in your trouser pocket; it looks ugly — or worse.

In a nut-shell: avoid, as best you can, all nervous mannerisms. If they are noticeable, the audience may concentrate on them, rather than listening to you. If that happens, you will be "whistling in the wind". You've "died".

Try too, to think about the words you are using. You

have decided broadly *what* you are going to say but, because you are speaking from notes rather than a script, you have not predetermined the actual words. Let your words be short, simple, everyday ones. use words that come readily to mind; DO NOT strive to find *impressive* words to use. Your purpose is to communicate your message, your enthusiasm, what you have to offer; not to show how clever you are.

And the communication process can almost always be improved by some form of visual aid. The Chinese have a proverb (of course): "I hear and forget; I see and I remember . . ."

Visual aids

There are two conflicting considerations relevant to the use of visual aids:

- they give the audience something interesting to look at and reinforce the spoken message; but
- they distract the audience's attention away from you.

The approach must therefore be, to use a visual aid when it *helps* to put across your message — and not, when it doesn't earn its place.

When making a presentation to a table-sized group of business people, there is much to be said for having a small white display board at which you can point. (The display board can incorporate a flip chart — sheets of ready-made illustrations.) But it must not need elaborate setting up, easels, etc. In a business situation, there may be no time for such preparation.

Alternatively, if you are talking to the local WI group, or lecturing to a group of your peers, an overhead projector is useful. This depends, of course, on the availability of the equipment. It also means that you must prepare your visual aid material in advance.

Avoid 35mm slides — they require a darkened room

and special equipment (and the talk becomes a slide show); avoid blackboards — they require you to turn your back on the audience (and get your hands all chalky); avoid films — for reasons of equipment and the need for a darkened room. Apart from the small display board, plus associated flip charts, which is ideal for the business presentation; and the overhead projector, which is ideal in a lecture type situation; the only other visual aid worth considering is a video cassette.

The main disadvantage of the video cassette is that, like the film, it wholly takes over the presentation role. The video ends, and the speaker than has to work hard to regain the audience's attention. And a video really only works in a business (or home) environment; it is inappropriate for, eg. the WI meeting.

It might have been possible to "get away with" amateur quality visual aids twenty years ago. But not today. Today, almost everyone has television and has been subjected to really first-class visual presentations. (Think of election reporting today compared with twenty years ago.) You will be expected to come up to the same high standard; if you can't, you would be wiser to give up any thoughts of using visual aids.

Whether an overhead projector slide, a flip chart, or a small display board, the same basic principles apply to the preparation of professional quality visual aids. These include:

- a visual aid should be . . . visual. Avoid using too many, or just, words; try to use a diagram whenever possible. If you must include words — as you often will — try to keep the number down to about 25.
- make your visual aid simple. Including too much information in a visual aid is counter-productive; if you want to put across a lot of detailed information, provide a hand-out. And make sure that each slide/chart/diagram has just a single, straight-forward

message. Multi-purpose slides don't work. Several simple visual aids are always better than one complicated one.
- design your visual aid attractively — think about how it looks. It needs to be almost a work of art — but steer clear of any actual pictures; it needs to be memorable — which comes from simplicity; it is best if colourful (most people have colour TV nowadays — not monochrome); and it MUST NOT LOOK AMATEURISH. (No wavy freehand lines, no scrawled writing, etc.)
- remove the distraction of the visual aid as soon as it has been on show long enough to be absorbed. *You* should be the main attraction. Don't let the visual aids take over.

And finally, in terms of visual aids, anything that you can leave with your audience — a handout, a brochure, a sample — is a lasting reminder of you; and that's good.

So — if you are asked to make a sales presentation, or to speak to the local WI, don't miss the opportunity. Forget your fears — they will actually help, not hinder. the more talks you give, the easier they become. Practice really does make . . . well, perhaps not perfect, but . . . better.

And a talk to several people can often be more productive than talking on a one-to-one basis. It can lead to even more sales. And that's what business is all about.

10
MONEY – AND RELATED MATTERS

We have already, in Chapter 2, looked at the question of raising capital for your mini-business. But start-up capital is not the only "money matter" you have to think about. You also need to give careful consideration to:

- the availability of government grants
- the need to keep accounts — and/or an accountant
- the need for insurance
- the impact of Income Tax
- the need to pay National Insurance contributions
- the relevance of Value Added Tax (VAT)
- your pension — existing or to come

To help you in this consideration, seek all the advice and help available. And, luckily, there is a lot.

First, you should collect all the government leaflets and booklets you can; they cover a vast range of matters which will have an effect on your mini-business; they are all free, and they are usually very helpful. An inevitably incomplete list of the relevant government publications which I have collected is:

Leaflet FB 30 *Self-employed?* (DHSS) — a guide to contributions and benefits.

Leaflet NI 255 *NI Contributions — Direct Debit* (DHSS) — the easy way to pay Class 2 or 3 contributions.

Leaflet NI 27A *NI for people with small earnings from self-employment* (DHSS)

Leaflet NI 41 *NI guide for the self-employed* (DHSS)
Leaflet NP 18 *Class 4 NI contributions* (DHSS)

Leaflet IR 57 *Thinking of Working for Yourself?* (IR)
Leaflet IR 28 *Starting in Business* (IR)

Leaflet 700 *The VAT Guide* (C&E)
Leaflet 700/1/87 *Should I be Registered for VAT?* (C&E)

Leaflet EAS 102 *The Enterprise Allowance Scheme Guide* — an Action for Jobs leaflet (MSC)

Leaflet PL 783 *Starting your own business — the practical steps* — an Action for Jobs leaflet (SFS)

Leaflet PL 818 *Accounting for a small firm* by Dennis F Millar — an Action for Jobs leaflet (DEmp)

Leaflet PL 819 *Marketing* by E G Wood — an Action for Jobs leaflet (DEmp)

The leaflets marked (DHSS) can be obtained from your local DHSS office (look in the telephone directory) or by post from Leaflets Unit, P O Box 21, Stanmore, Middlesex HA7 1AT.

Leaflets marked (IR) — for Inland Revenue — can be obtained from your nearest Inspector of Taxes' office.

Leaflets marked (C&E) — for Customs & Excise — can be obtained from local offices.

Leaflets marked (MSC), (SFS) or (DEmp) can be obtained from local offices of the Department of Employment (eg Job Centres) or by post from Small Firms Division, Department of Employment, Steel House, Tothill Street, London SW1H 9NF, or by phoning 100 and asking for Freephone Enterprise.

Government publications aside, there are also many very helpful publications, available free, from the major banks and from CoSIRA — the Council for Small Industries in Rural Areas. (Contact CoSIRA at one of their local offices, or at the head office at 141 Castle Street, Salisbury, Wilts SP1 3TP — and ask for a copy of their booklet *Developing a small business — a checklist and business plan.*)

Grants

Helpful leaflets aside, one of the most useful recent things that Government has done for mini-businesses is the Enterprise Allowance Scheme (hereafter EAS). this applies however, only to those budding mini-business people who are in receipt of unemployment benefit. That said, it is an admirable "cushion" scheme for those who are eligible.

At the time of writing, the EAS pays £40 per week for up to 52 weeks, to an eligible person who starts up a new, small business. The grant is to supplement the receipts of the new business while it is becoming established.

There are, inevitably, strict conditions for eligibility for the EAS. The most important, apart from the unemployment benefit condition already referred to, is that it must be NEW. If your business is in any way already started you will probably be ineligible. It is most important therefore that you check with the Enterprise Allowance staff before doing anything about starting up.

Another important condition of acceptance into the EAS is that you can show that you have at least £1000 available for investment in the business in the first 12 months. This can be in the form of a loan or an overdraft though; you don't have to have that much personal capital.

Other conditions include the requirements that the business be small (you should not propose initially to employ more than 20 workers — which is no problem for a mini-business as defined in this book); it should be a full-time business (at least 36 hours per week); it must be "suitable" (eg a photographer specialising in pornographic pictures would not be eligible); it must be based in Britain; and, obviously, it has to be approved.

The first step towards an EAS grant is to contact the relevant staff at your local Jobcentre. You will be invited to attend an information session. And you will get a copy of Leaflet EAS 102, referred to above. Thereafter there will be forms to fill in and interviews to survive. They will want to see your business plan. And then you will be able to start up your mini-business with financial support from the Scheme.

Another major "plus-point" for the EAS is that accepted participants get the benefit of free advice from business experts. You get three separate one-to-one interviews with professional advisers such as marketing experts, solicitors or accountants; these initial interviews are free of charge. You can have further consultations — but not for free. And there are business clubs which you can join.

Many successful mini-businesses have already been started under the auspices of the EAS. Yours could be the next. If you are eligible, explore the possibilities.

Accounts

As we have said, one of the things that the EAS will require of you, is a business plan. And certainly, if you are to seek eg, the EAS £1000 capital as a loan from a bank, they too will require to see one. And following on from your business plan there will be the need to keep accounts. If you are going to run your own mini-business — whether under the EAS, or in early retirement, or as a part-time activity in support of either income or pension — you will certainly need to keep some sort of accounts.

You need accounts to tell whether your mini-business is doing well or badly. You need them for the Inspector of Taxes too (*see* below). The idea of keeping accounts worries some people. And undoubtedly, keeping accounts entails a certain amount of careful effort. But accounts need not be frightening — so long as they are accurate and kept up-to-date. Never let yourself fall behind.

Simple accounts need be no more than a record of income and expenditure. The most convenient, simple way of doing this is in a book whose pages are divided in two: columns on the left for income; columns on the right for expenditure. (Accountants will refer to income as *debits* (Dr), and expenditure as *credits* (Cr); but this is unnecessarily confusing unless you are going for a full double-entry accounting system. Initially at least, I suggest you think merely in terms of income and expenditure.)

It is particularly helpful though if, when keeping your accounting records, the income and expenditure items can be further subdivided (analysed) to show whence the money comes or goes. This makes it easier to prepare the final accounts; it is the system I have used myself for some years; and it has proved perfectly adequate. *Figure 10.1* shows a (fictional) version of my recent accounts.

You will also find it very helpful — and required by the EAS — to open a separate bank account for your mini-business. You should then be able to reconcile your bank statements with your accounts book.

Depending on the size of your mini-business it will probably be sensible occasionally to consult — or regularly use the services of — an accountant. Without doubt, an accountant can give you helpful advice on starting up any mini-business. (*See,* for instance, the significance of start-up dates, referred to on page 192 below, in relation to income tax.) But the smaller operations may not need the regular services of one.

A helpful rule of thumb is that as soon as your mini-business becomes large enough to entail VAT registration (*see* below), you would probably be wise to employ an accountant. (Only if you operate as a limited company however, are you *legally required* to employ one.) If your profit is in the two or three thousand pounds per year bracket, you probably don't need one. In between, you must think carefully — explore the

Figure 10.1 An extract from a simple, but often adequate, accounts book, showing how income and expenditure can easily be analysed. (As successfully used by the author — and fictionally representing his writing accounts).

Date	Item	Income	Books	Articles	Lectures	Sales	Other	
June	Run. Total 95/6 BF	1021 13	500 -	170 -	150 -	89 90	111 23	
1/6	Foulsham Royalties	363 17	363 17					
3/6	Article - WMFdy A89012	35 -		35 -				
6/6	Middleton Talk + Sales	57 93			30 -	27 93		

Date	Item	Expend.	Post	Research	Travel	Stat'y	Tel.	Other
June	Run Total 95/6 BF	261 33	25 94	29 99	86 14	12 -	21 04	86 22
1/6	Post: Foulsham WHA Flw	66	66					
2/6	Visit WHA	12 66			12 66			
3/6	Menu Foulsham	1 -					1 -	
6/6	Travel Middleton Talk	25 -			25 -			
	Pay L. June	40 -						40
7/6	Paper (spty) + Pen refills	7 24		5 99		1 25		

186

charges of your friendly local accountant — and make up your own mind.

Another aspect of a mini-business operation, related to the keeping of accounts, is the issuing of invoices. (In simple terms, if you do something for someone, or supply them with something, you may need to bill them.) Again, to the inexperienced, the issuing of invoices is a worry; it need not be.

An invoice need be no more than a typed statement, preferably on the headed notepaper used for the mini-business. It should be dated; it is useful to give it a reference number; it should identify the organisation to whom it is addressed; and it should be very clear in the amount that you are seeking to be paid.

On the few occasions when I have to invoice someone — most publishers and editors don't require invoices — I use my (second-quality, less-expensive) headed notepaper and a form of words like:

INVOICE

31 February 1993

XYZ Consultants Ltd
23 High Street
Anytown   Mudshire   MX9 99X

INVOICE   Ref: GW.00032/93

To:

30 Feb — One-day training course
          Technical Letter and Report Writing
                    Agreed fee £000.00

          TOTAL DUE   £000.00

              (No VAT Registration)

And, generally, I believe in invoicing immediately I have completed a job.

Always keep a copy of your invoices, and check back through them at fairly frequent intervals to make sure they have been paid. In fact, a regular routine for checking on unpaid invoices is essential. One system is to send out monthly "Statements" — ie summaries of invoices and payments — but this may well be unnecessarily complex for a smaller mini-business.

My own approach is to give a client/customer to the end of the month after the date of the invoice — and then phone my contact. With the small scale of my invoicing, this works very well.

If you issue more than a mere handful of invoices, you will find it essential to keep a *record* of your invoices. This need be no more than a list, in numerical order, identifying:

- reference number of invoice
- date issued
- to whom issued (firm, etc)
- amount of invoice
- amount paid
- date of payment

Kept up to date, this will help you to identify unpaid accounts quickly.

Insurance

Even for a mini-business, you will probably need at least some insurance other than purely personal. The mere fact that you are pursuing a business within the confines of your home may mean that you need to amend your existing house insurance. This will depend on the extent of the "changed use". You may need to take out professional indemnity insurance — against giving incorrect advice, for instance; and even if working basically alone, it may be prudent to have employer's liability insurance in case an accident occurs while a friend is "helping you out".

Depending on the nature of your mini-business, you may also need some or all of the following:

- employer's liability
- motor insurance
- equipment insurance
- fire insurance — for premises
- insurance against theft — of goods or money
- insurance of goods in transit
- credit insurance — against non-payment
- professional indemnity insurance
- product liability insurance

The trouble with insurance is that you never really accept that you need it — until something goes wrong. And then it's too late to do anything about it. You almost certainly need some; just don't get talked into taking out more than you need.

Before extending your present life and/or property insurance to cover your mini-business therefore, consult an insurance broker. (Get a list of reputable brokers from The British Insurance and Investment Brokers Association, 14 Bevis Marks, London EC3A 7NT.) There are packages of insurance supposedly covering all the needs of a small business; you will probably want less. So negotiate.

Income Tax

Income Tax is something that needs to be carefully thought about too. Whilst it is illegal — and immoral — to *evade* tax, it is eminently sensible to *avoid* unnecessary taxation. In other words, you should avail yourself of every legal relaxation or tax-reducing opportunity.

(A classic instance of this, to which we shall refer

again later, is the tax-efficient purchase of a self-employed pension. By buying yourself a pension, you *avoid* paying tax on the premiums — with certain limitations.)

Much of your expenditure on your mini-business will be deductible, ie, no tax will need to be paid on it. This includes in my case, for instance, the rental charge on a telephone line used partly for domestic and partly for business purposes. I also deduct — with the agreement of the Inspector of Taxes — all my postage expenses, work-related travel expenses, and the cost of business stationery. The Inspector also allows me a portion of the overhead domestic costs for the partial use of one room.

Working from home, as I do, it is important to take care over the use of a room. Were I to claim tax relief on the *exclusive* use of a room, I could be liable to Capital Gains Tax (CGT) on a similar proportion of the total capital value of the family home.

(Profit on the sale of the main family home — ie, as opposed to an extra "holiday cottage" — is not usually liable to CGT.)

It pays to seek advice from an accountant — or direct from your local Inspector of Taxes, who is often very helpful — about appropriate ways of avoiding unnecessary taxation in your mini-business. The Inspector will be willing to agree with you, in advance, which items are tax deductible.

Capital items are different. Were I to buy a new computer, that is not directly deductible against income. It is a capital item. As a capital expenditure 25 per cent is currently chargeable against income in the first year; the remaining 75 per cent of the cost of the capital equipment is then carried over to the next year. If, in year 2, I then buy a new printer, the cost of this is added to the remaining 75 per cent of the computer — and 25 per cent of the total is eligible to set against income. And so on.

This is clearer in an example. In 1989 I buy a computer for £1000; £250 of this is set against income as an expense in that year. In 1990, there is a carried over capital expenditure of the remaining £750; I now buy a printer for £500 giving a total capital expenditure of £750 + £500 = £1250. Of that £1250, I can claim 25%, ie £313, as a 1990 expense; and I can carry forward the remaining capital sum of £937 to 1991. And so on.

Capital items aside, there are other aspects of income tax that some smaller mini-businesses might be wise to think about. Maybe your income can be kept down to such a level that you don't pay tax at all.

No income tax is payable on several thousands of pounds of annual income. Every person is entitled to an allowance before tax is levied. (Let us, for the moment, ignore the matter of National Insurance.) In tax year 1989-90 a married man is allowed to earn £4375 (from *all* sources — see next paragraph) wholly free of income tax. And if a man employs his wife to help in the mini-business — and she must actually work for him, "on paper" employment is not allowed — he could pay her £2785 without either of them being liable to income tax. (But see below).

In other words, husband and wife working together could earn £7160 in 1989-90 before starting to pay income tax. But in such circumstances, the husband and wife team should take care there is no other income — from the state old age pension, from a company pension, or from bank deposit accounts etc. — before assuming they are safe from taxation.

But we cannot continue to ignore the effect of National Insurance — which we review in more detail below.

Our mini-business husband would in fact be unwise to pay his wife the full, tax-allowable, £2785 mentioned above. He would be better advised to pay her only

£2235 — thereby avoiding the necessity for her to pay National Insurance contributions. (The National Insurance "threshold" in 1989/90 was £43 per week, £2236 per annum.)

Back now to our consideration merely of income tax. Earning more than the £7160 is, in any case, not the end of the world. Tax on each pound above that level is only 25 per cent. Of the couple working together, the husband would need to make another £20,700 — from all sources — to move into the higher tax rate bracket (currently 40 per cent). Again 1989-90 rates.

(The income tax regulations have now changed though. Since 1990 the wife is treated as a separate individual with her own personal tax allowance and basic tax rate band. But the point about the wife's National Insurance contributions is still applicable.)

A further income tax point to bear in mind is that . . . there is no PAYE for the self-employed. As a self-employed mini-business-person you will pay tax in arrears, under Schedule D, based on your profits in your accounting year which ends during the previous tax year.

The somewhat tortuous phrasing at the end of the previous paragraph is important because, at start-up, income tax is assessed for up to three years on the basis of the first full year's profit. And it is this first year basis which explains why you should perhaps consult an accountant before deciding on the start date of your first year of business. In your first year profits are likely to be lower than those expected in subsequent years (or can be held down, eg by judicious purchasing of stocks) you can make substantial tax savings. This is best explained by an example.

Example: Consider a business starting in the Spring of 1989. Once established, annual profits are expected to be £10,000 and rising, but in the first year they will only be £5,000 —because of stocking up, etc.

Let the starting date of the business be 6 March 1989. Annual profits by accounting year are therefore:

Year ending	Profit	
5 March 1990	£5,000	
5 March 1991	£10,000	
5 March 1992	£11,000	£26,000 (to 1992)

The basis of the tax assessments will be:

Tax year	Basis	Amount	
1988/89	Actual, £5,000 x 1/12	£ 417	
1989/90	First year's profit	£ 5,000	
1990/91	Profit as in accounts ending in previous tax year	£ 5,000	
1991/92	Ditto	£10,000	£20,417

Now let the starting date of the business be 6 May 1989. Profits by accounting year are the same — but the accounting year end now falls into a later tax year. Thus:

Year ending	Profit	
5 May 1990	£5,000	
5 May 1991	£10,000	
5 May 1992	£11,000	£26,000 (to 1992)

The basis of the tax assessments will now be very different:

Tax year	Basis	Amount	
1989/90	Actual, £5,000 x 11/12	£ 4,583	
1990/92	First year's profit	£ 5,000	
1991/92	Previous year	£ 5,000	£14,583
1992/93	Previous year	£10,000	

By deferring the accounting year start date by two months, the mini-business has avoided tax on £5834. A very significant — and perfectly legal — saving.

But income tax is not the only tax you will have to think about. There are also National Insurance contributions — to which we have already referred. They too are a tax, specifically on income.

National Insurance contributions

As a self-employed person below the age of 60 for a woman or 65 for a man, you are required, by law, to pay National Insurance (hereafter NI) contributions.

Basically, a self-employed person pays what are known as Class 2 contributions. These are a fixed amount and are payable weekly. (in 1989-90 Class 2 NI contributions were £4.25 per week.) You can make arrangements to pay these contributions by direct debit from your mini-business bank account — and this method is strongly recommended. (If you forget to buy the individual stamps for a few weeks, the cost of "catching up" can soon mount up.)

There is one significant exception (other than age) from having to pay NI self-employed contributions. If your estimated earnings for a year, after deducting agreed expenses, are less than a set amount, the Department of Social Services will issue you with a specific Small Earnings Exception certificate. (But there are disadvantages too, in not paying Class 2 NI contributions: for instance, your retirement pension and/or your widow's pension may be reduced. Exception may not be worth obtaining.) In 1989-90, the Small Earnings Exception certificate was issued for earnings of less than £2350 per annum.

If your estimated earnings (less expenses) are very small — less than £800 in 1989-90 — you must still apply for exception from liability for Class 2 contributions. But you will not be given a certificate. Instead, you will simply be advised that your earnings are too small for payment of contributions. This advice remains valid until your circumstances change; you do not need to renew it. This situation is particularly relevant to those who decide to establish their mini-businesses in their spare time before changing to full time operation.

Part-time mini-business operators may also be excepted from Class 2 NI contributions by virtue of their other, wage-related, contributions. Every employed person has NI Class 1 contributions deducted at source by their employer. If your full-time pay is so large that you pay the maximum NI contribution on it, you will not have to pay further contributions in respect of your part-time activities.

But there is more to come. Your Class 2 NI contributions suffice only for earnings up to a specified level — £5050 in 1989-90. If your self-employed earnings exceed that amount, you will also have to pay Class 4 NI contributions.

Class 4 NI contributions are assessed and collected by the Inland Revenue, together with your Schedule D income tax. In 1989-90 they amount to 6.3 per cent on earnings from £5050 to £16900. The good news is that there is an upper limit to the total NI contributions (in all Classes, taken together) that anyone has to pay. In 1989-90 this total contribution figure was £1550.25.

This latter point will be of particular importance to anyone in a similar position to myself. I am "retained" for a number of days' waged employement per year; for this work I am treated as employed and I have to pay Class 1 NI contributions (a maximum of £29.25 per week — 9% of the maximum £325 per week) in respect of the weeks during which I work. (My employers have to pay a further employers' contribution too — but that is no concern of mine.) I also pay my weekly Class 2 contributions, of course; and it looks as though, at the end of the year, I may have to pay Class 4 contributions as well. But irrespective of how many or which NI Classes I pay under, I know that my total annual contributions will not exceed £1550.25. Phew!

All these features of the NI system are explained in the leaflets mentioned at the start of this chapter. Make sure you get up-to-date copies. By the time this book is published, my figures will inevitably be out of date; they are merely to give a "feel" for the system.

The "good news" about the NI system is that once you reach the age limits specified above (60 for women, 65 for men), you no longer pay any contributions at all. And that's an important factor to all mini-business-persons working in their "retirement".

Another tax which may be an important factor in your mini-business is Value Added Tax — VAT.

Value Added Tax (VAT)

First, the good news. You do not have to concern yourself with VAT if your annual turnover — NOTE: not earnings nor profit, but "total throughput of money" — is less than a specified figure. In 1989-90 the VAT limit was £23,600. In fact, the rules are slightly more specific. You must register for VAT as soon as the turnover in any *quarter* exceeds a rounded £8000 (in 1989-90).

If your mini-business is involved with buying and selling things, or making goods with expensive materials (ie, "adding value"), you will soon reach a turnover exceeding the VAT limit. But if you are a writer, for example, your turnover will not be vastly different from your total earnings. And few writers earn £23,600 per annum.

Before you start to congratulate yourself on not having to worry about VAT, or cursing your luck because you do, think a little further. There may be advantages in being VAT registered. Some people whose turnover is below the VAT limit, register voluntarily. Before registration though, it is necessary to satisfy Customs & Excise that one's activities "constitute a business for VAT purposes."

I am not VAT registered; unsurprisingly, I do not (yet) earn £23,600 per year from my writing. (Move over, Jeffrey Archer.) I occasionally wonder whether I should seek voluntary registration though.

Each time I buy ribbons for my printer and paper to feed into it — both of which are significant items of my expenditure — I pay 15 per cent VAT over the retail price. This is perfectly fair; it is a form of taxation; we all pay VAT on most things we buy (apart from food and books and a few other items).

If I were registered for VAT though, I would have to keep my accounts so that the VAT element in the cost of my printer ribbons and paper was recorded separately. Then, I would also have to require publishers, editors, consultants — anyone for whom I work — to add a VAT element on to their payments to me.

Thus, if my next annual royalty payment from XYZ Books were to be £100, this would be increased to £115. (With some publishers, the royalty is paid without the VAT addition, and the author has to raise an invoice specifically for the VAT. That is, they pay me the £100, and I bill them for the extra £15, which only then do they pay to me). XYZ Books would declare — to the Customs and Excise — their VAT payment to me. And they would claim reimbursement of that amount.

I would then have to declare that I had received £15 VAT and balance that receipt against, say, £4.50 of VAT paid on a £30 purchase of paper (a total price of £34.50). And I would have to account for, and pay to the Customs & Excise VAT office the difference between the £15 and the £4.50 — ie £10.50. But note: if VAT-registered, I am in fact £4.50 better off than if not VAT-registered. (If not registered, I would pay the full £34.50 for the paper but only receive £100 in royalties from XYZ Books.

The VAT system requires that you keep rather more complicated accounts than the simple cash-book type of account that I have described earlier. But the extra complication is not great. All you need do is include a further two columns on both income and expenditure sides for the VAT element and the net figure.

Thus, for a simple cash-book system where no invoices are involved — eg for someone who is only a writer, earning royalties and unbilled publication fees — the income side would need columns headed:

    Gross receipt   (eg £115 from XYZ Books)
    VAT   (ie £ 15 output tax)
    Net receipt   (= £100 net royalty)

and any subdivision of the receipts by source should then relate only to the net figures.

Similarly, the expenditure side, would need columns headed:

    Gross cost   (eg £34.50 for paper)
    VAT   (ie £ 4.50 input tax)
    Net cost   (= £30.00 "reduced" cost)

and again, any subdivision of expenses should relate to the net figures only.

Once VAT registered, you will need to report to, and settle the VAT account with, the Customs & Excise office quarterly. To do this, you must keep copies of all documents supporting payments to yourself — usually your own invoices; and the payments you make — usually others' invoices, but also cash slips from shop tills etc. It is best to keep all these pieces of paper in date order.

(A tip. Many sales cash slips from retail shops merely record the total price paid. They do not separate the net cost and the VAT element. You must do this yourself. *Do not deduct 15 per cent.* If something costs £100 net, the dealer adds on 15% and charges you £115. Fifteen percent of £115 is £17.25; if you deduct that you get a net cost of £97.75 — which is not correct. To get the *correct* net cost, you need to divide the gross cost by 1.15. Thus, £115 divided by 1.15 equals a correct £100. Using a pocket calculator it is not difficult to divide by 1.15 — no more difficult than determining the 15% which you might have thought was necessary. And, of course, if the VAT rate changes to 17% you need to divide by 1.17 and so on.)

As already recommended (earlier in this chapter), once you get into the business of VAT registration and accounting, it is probably time to avail yourself of the services of an accountant. (Don't pay the accountants an annual retaining fee though; pay for their services as you need them, by the hour.)

Once you have committed yourself to using the services of an accountant, don't just sit back and leave it all to them. Both in respect of VAT accounts and "ordinary" accounts, the more you can do yourself, the smaller will be the accountant's bill.

Clearly, you *could* just dump a box full of receipts and copy invoices on the accountant's desk and let them sort it out. But it will cost you. It is far better to present the accountant with neatly kept account books, receipts and expense slips filed in date order, and well-recorded invoices. Given well-kept papers, accountants' services will always be cheaper.

Pensions

And finally, in this review of some of the financial considerations which affect every mini-business — pensions. There are two Important Questions to be asked about pensions:

1 Will your mini-business in any way affect a pension already earned, and possibly even being paid?
2 Can you arrange for a pension based on your mini-business earnings?

And the answers are "good" in both cases.

Until the 1989 Budget, any mini-business worker in the United Kingdom lost out badly in the first five years of ("normal") retirement. Men aged 65 to 69 and women aged 60 to 64 were able to earn no more than £75 per week without penalty; over £75 a week and the state pension was reduced on a graduated scale. (The way to avoid this penalty was to defer drawing the state pension until either the earnings dropped or the pensioner reached the upper age limit.) But in the 1989 Budget, the earnings limit for pensioners was totally abolished.

Today, no matter what you earn from your mini-business, your state pension is unaffected.

(It might still be worth deferring the drawing of your state pension though: to reduce your liability to income tax. Like any other form of income, your state pension is taxable; the reason some people pay no tax on their pension is because they have no other source of income — and their pension is less than the tax allowances available to them. And the basic state pension is increased for each year it is deferred.)

You may also be entitled to what is known as an occupational pension. (An occupational pension is one which you have earned, and/or towards which you have made financial contributions, in respect of your employment.) Such a pension will not be affected by the earnings of your mini-business. What you earn in your retirement is no concern of your past employers.

This also applies to pensioners of both Central and Local Government; a civil servant's occupational pension may be paid by the state, but it is not a state pension as such.

The answer to Important Question Number 1 is therefore a definite — and welcome — NO.

There is then the Important Question (Number 2) of whether you can earn yourself a pension based on the profits of your mini-business. And again the answer is the welcome one — YES.

The income tax regulations allow any self-employed person to invest up to 17.5 per cent of *relevant earnings* (which are effectively the same as taxable income less capital allowances) in a personal pension scheme. Within that limit, however much you invest in a pension scheme is allowable as pre-tax expenditure. In other words, you save the tax on whatever you invest in your pension.

(Thus, if you invest £100 in a personal pension policy, at a time when the basic tax rate is 25%, you will eventually have £25 less tax to pay than you would otherwise have done. Or . . . you only pay £75 to get £100 worth of value.)

The 17.5 per cent "tax allowance" increases with your age; if you are over 50 you can invest 20 per cent; the allowance is even greater for those over 70.

Having invested your tax-free earnings in a self-employed pension fund, you may then start drawing your pension at any age you choose — and agree with the company arranging the pension — between 50 and 75. (But think carefully before you start taking your pension too soon. It will be worth considerably more if you delay drawing it. The longer your money stays invested, the more it earns — and the more the total fund grows.)

When you start drawing the pension, you can immediately withdraw 25 per cent of your pension fund as a tax-free lump sum. But, of course, you will be liable to pay tax on the pension payments thereafter.

Clearly, there are tax advantages in investing in a personal pension: how great these advantages are, will depend on the respective rates of taxation when you purchase the pension and when you draw it. And, of course, it is good to know that when you eventually stop running your mini-business, you will continue to draw a pension from your present endeavours.

Personal pension schemes are offered by most insurance companies and many other financial organisations. It will pay you to shop around. Your bank manager will often be able to advise you. But whatever you do, start buying a pension as soon as possible. The earlier you start, the better the terms.

Manage your money wisely. The main object of your mini-business is to make money. (If not, apart from having fun, what for?) Work hard to make it pay; keep good financial records; avoid unnecessary tax — but never try to evade it; and plan for the future. That's a **successful** mini-business. Go to it.

INDEX

Accommodation options for mini-businesses, 65-69
Accountant, need for, 185, 199
Accounts, 184
Activity of mini-business, 11
Advertisements, targeting, 126
Advertising, 111-131
Allowances, tax, 191
Ambition, Mini-business, 18
Amstrad (computer, word-processor), 74, 77, 102
Answering machine, telephone, 73
Appearance of letters, 102
Articles for the press, 130
Assessment of market, 28, 30, 34

Borrowing money, 30
Boss, be your own, 60
Briefcase, contents of, 107
Brochures, 120, 180
Buyers' requirements, 94
Business card, 106, 108
— image, 101
— objectives, 32
— plan, 25-45
— —, capital resources, 35
— —, contents of, 28
— —, reasons for, 29-32

Capital for mini-business, 28, 35
Capital Gains Tax (CGT), 190

Cards, business, 106, 108
Case Studies, 23, 46, 90, 109, 132, 150, 164
Cash flow forecast, 28, 41
Chair, office, 73
Chart, time, 54
Clothes, importance of, 106
Commitment, 18, 25, 98
Communicate, How To, 19
Communication by computer, 85
Computer, basic principles of, 74 (and Fig 4.2)
—, choosing, 78
—, office, 74
—, programs, 80
Confidence, gaining, 153
—, over-, 176
Contacts, importance and value of, 112
CoSIRA, 182
Craft of Writing Articles, The, 132

Database programs, 80
Definition of a mini-business, 9
Delivering a talk, 175
Desk-top publishing programs, 81
Diaries, importance of, 52, 107

80/20 rule, 56

Electronic mail
  ("e-mail"), 85
Enterprise Allowance
  Scheme (EAS), 183
Equipment (and premises),
  63-89
Exclusivity, 98

Family relationships,
  15, 50, 51
Fax, 86
Files and filing, 73, 87
Financing of a mini-
  business, 19
Freepost, 125
Furniture, office, 73

Grants, Government, for
  mini-businesses, 183
Gunning, Robert, 145

Handouts, lecture, 100, 180
HIBA mnemonic, 115, 138,
  157
Holidays, 15, 49
House-cum-workshop, 69

Image, business, 101
—, personal, 106, 153-156
Impressive writing, avoid,
  149
Income Tax, 181, 189
Insurance for mini-
  businesses, 188
Investment, check on, 30
Invoices, 187

KISS mnemonic, 127, 135,
  145

Layout, brochure, 121
—, letters, 103
  (and Fig 5.1)
Lecture handouts, 100
Letterhead, 102
Letters, appearance of, 102
—, layout of, 103
  (and Fig 5.1)
—, sales, 114
—, structure of, 115, 138
—, titles for, 139
Letter-writing, 135-139
Limited company, 27
Lists, 56
—, mailing, 124

Mailing lists, 124
—, mechanics of, 124
Mannerisms, avoid, 177
Market, assessing, 28, 30, 34
Marketing, 111-131
—, policy, 96
Mini-business
  Accounts, 184
  Advertising, 111-131
  Ambition needed for, 18
  Business plan for, 25-45
  Computing needs of, 74
  Financing, 19, 35
  Furniture, 73
  Insurance, 188
  Life in a, 13
  Money matters, 181-202

Mini-business
  Monitoring performance,
    45, 57
  Objectives, 32
  Pensions, 200
  Personal characteristics
    needed for, 15
  Premises and equipment,
    63-89
  Sales letters, 114-118
  Selling, 93-108, 153-163
  Spare-time, 21, 184
  Targets, 53-60
  Timing for start-up,
    19, 192
  Types, 11, 25
Modern English Usage, 144
Money, borrowing, 30
—, making, 14, 25, 41
—, matters, 181-202
Monitoring mini-business
  performance, 45, 57
Motivation, 13, 60

National Insurance
  Contributions (NIC)
  10, 22, 39, 181, 191, 194
Notes for a talk, 172, 175

Objectives, business, 32
Office equipment, 71-89
Operating systems,
  computer, 77
Overheads, 38

Packaging

Paper, quality for
  letters, 102
Partnerships, 26
Pension (Self-employed),
  190, 200
Performance checks, 32, 45
Permission, planning, 63-65
Personal image, 106, 153-156
Photocopier, 85
Plan, business, 25-45
Planning considerations
  relating to
  premises, 63-65
—, your letters, 135
— —, your time, 52
Policy, marketing, 96
Polishing your writing, 148
Post Office, 125
Practicing a talk, 173
Premises for mini-
  business, 63-69
Preparing a talk, 170
—, notes for a talk, 172
Presence, 153-156
Presentation at sales
  interview, 116
—, to groups, 167-180
Press releases, 128-131
Priorities, 56-60
Product, faith in, 157
Profit margin, 96
—, plan, 28, 37
Programs, computer, 80
Projecting your voice, 176
Purpose of letter, 136, 139
Pushiness, need for, 16

Qualities personal, of mini-business-person, 15

RAM, 75
Random access memory (RAM), 75
Reader of letter, importance of, 136
Reader's Digest, 114
Reading aloud, 146
Retirement, 19, 50, 184

Sales letters, 114-118
Salesmanship, 93-108, 153-163
Samples, 107, 161, 180
Scope for chosen mini-business, 12
Security in a mini-business, 14
Selling basis, 94
Sentence length, 142
"Short" writing, 141-145
Sole trader, 26, 33
Spare-time mini-business, 21, 184
Spreadsheet programs, 81
"Stagger through" for talk, 173
Start-up date for a mini-business, 19, 192
Status from a mini-business, 14
Structure for letters, 138
— —, sales letters (HIBA), 115

— —, talk, 170
3x rule, 158, 160, 171
Talk, delivering, 175
—, giving a, 167-180
—, structuring a, 170
—, visual aids for, 178
Targeting advertisements, 126
Targets, work, 56-60
Tax allowances, 191
—, Capital Gains, (CGT), 190
—, Income, 181, 189
Telephone, 72
—, follow-ups to letters, 118
Thinking before talking, 168
Time chart, 54
— log, keeping, 53
—, using, 49-61
Timing of mini-business start-up, 19, 192
Titles for letters, 139
Types of mini-business, 11, 25
Typewriter, 71
Townsend, Robert, 25

Underlining, 117
Up the Organisation, 25

VAT (Value Added Tax), 36, 39, 43, 181, 196
Visual aids for a talk, 178
Voice projection, 176

Wage-slavery, 13, 49
Wibberley, Mary, 18
Word processing, 77, 80

Workload, check on, 32
Workshop-cum-house, 69
Work-Schedule, 54
Writing articles, 130

—, clear and simple, 141
—, improving, tips for, 146
— letters, 135-149
— press releases, 128-131